DESERTS
Deserts

WHITE STAR
PUBLISHERS

Cover
The winding dunes so characteristic of the Sahara desert rise in all their impressive majesty.
Photograph by Marie-Anne Chamel/ Agence Freestyle

Back cover - top
Three gemsboks (Oryx gazela) run lightly over the dazzling surface of the large depression of Etosha Pan, in Namibia.
Photograph by Jen and Des Bartlett/ Bruce Colman

Back cover - bottom
The unsettling presence of the Tuareg lends a special fascination to the silent expanses of the Algerian Sahara.
Photograph by Angelo Tondini/ Focus Team

1 The high dunes of the Mehedjebat Erg in Algeria are one of the most stupendous examples of the creativity of the wind, which accumulates enormous quantities of sand and builds spectacular, ever-changing formations.

2-3 This is the Chebbi Erg in Morocco. Although the Sahara is commonly believed to be an endless expanse of dunes, sandy areas cover only about twenty percent of its surface.

DESERTS

Text
Marco Ferrari

Editorial production
Valeria Manferto De Fabianis

Graphic design
Anna Galliani

Map
Cristina Franco

Translation
A.B.A. S.r.l., Milan, Italy

Contents

4-5 Gebel Musa, traditionally associated with the Biblical Mount Sinai, where Moses received the Ten Commandments from God, is located in the southern Sinai desert. Near Gebel Musa is the monastery of St. Catherine, which dates back to the 6th century AD.

6-7 Considered a sacred mountain by the aborigines, Uluru, or Ayers Rock, as the colonists called it, is one of the most spectacular monoliths in the Australian desert. 867 meters high and 9 kilometers wide, it juts up from the center of the continent, surrounded by arid, flat earth.

8-9 A group of oryx works its way up the dunes of Sussusvlei in Namibia. Long and narrow, the Namib desert is extremely arid, as the atmospheric conditions and the ocean currents along the coast of southern Africa prevent moisture from penetrating the interior.

© 1996, 2003 White Star S.r.l.
Via C. Sassone, 22/24
13100 Vercelli, Italy
www.whitestar.it

ISBN 88-8095-941-7

REPRINTS:
2 3 4 5 6   08 07 06 05 04

Printed in Italy by Grafiche Industriali, Foligno.

INTRODUCTION

The desert. Man has always had a contradictory relationship with the scorching stretches of sand and barren rock that dot his planet. For some, these places seem distant, hostile and perilous, while others are drawn to and fascinated by them for reasons they cannot explain. Seemingly lifeless but nevertheless seductive, the desert has traditionally been a true testing ground for those in need of experience and contemplation. Many of the great men of the past (foremost among whom were Abraham, Jesus and Mohammed, founders of monotheistic religions who were born and lived in the desert) have had powerful experiences in its lifeless sands, living perhaps on locusts and wild honey.

The desert is thus a true symbol of the harshness of life - but only for man. In fact, beyond its image of complete desolation, like most parts of the planet deserts contain dozens and dozens, if not hundreds, of living beings, plants and animals who call the desert their home. The conditions they encounter have been extremely severe, perhaps the most terrible that life can offer on this planet. First among them is the scarcity or absolute lack of water.

This precious commodity, which is abundant (although not available for use) even in the "cold deserts" of the planet's polar regions, may fall only rarely in true deserts. Then there is the heat of the sun. Unscreened by a sheltering layer of clouds, the rays of the sun blaze down mercilessly, burning away the few drops of water that the living creatures below need to srvive. Why then, have so many species chosen the desert as their more or less permanent home? Those who have chosen to live in the desert have done so for a very simple reason - in these inhospitable expanses there are very few who could constitute a threat, and perhaps even fewer animals or plants capable of robbing them of the food or sun necessary for their survival. Thus, deserts may be considered a refuge from one of the great forces shaping evolution - competition. This, the extreme severity of the environment and the landscape, the harsh conditions of life, the austerity of an ecosystem reduced to the bone, is what makes the desert so fascinating.

10 top *Several centuries ago the Tuareg, a nomadic people of Berber origins, created a great empire that included a portion of eastern Africa. Even the city of Timbuktu, which was once an extremely important commercial center as well as a fulcrum for the diffusion of Arab culture, was founded by the Tuareg in the 11th century.*

10 bottom *The tribes which inhabit the Sahara are often quite independent from central governments and jealously preserve their traditional usages and customs. For example, even though the Tuareg are technically Muslims, Tuareg women do not wear the veil and are in fact autonomous, acting as the caretakers of Tuareg traditions and cultural heritage. Even the social status of tribal members is matrilineal, that is determined by female descent.*

11 *A great dune seems to hang over a small caravan of Tuareg. The caravan routes in the desert follow paths that are centuries old, dating back to the times when the nomads ambushed caravans of dromedaries or else offered their services as guides through the dunes and treacherous weather conditions.*

Although they appear ancient, almost eternal, deserts have not always covered such a vast area. Where do they come from, and what keeps them alive, so to speak? Numerous factors play a part in creating deserts. It all depends on position, proximity to or distance from mountains, the substratum, and, of course, precipitation. Inextricably intertwined, these environmental factors contribute not only to the birth, but also to the structure, life and "body" of the area. In essence, all deserts are the legacy of complex events of the past, with the great glacial periods playing some of the most important roles. Although these phenomena appear distant in both time and space, the great ice caps captured enormous quantities of water which would otherwise have been able to generate enough atmospheric humidity to transform the climate of the Earth. As the ice age loosened its grip, water flowed into the oceans, and from there by means of the water cycle it passed into the continental interiors, where the expanses of rock and sand greatly decreased.

Another impressively slow and grandiose phenomenon, the birth of mountains, also influenced the creation of deserts. For example, when the Himalayas took form about 70 million years ago, after India crashed into the continent of Asia, the interior was cut off from the moist ocean currents, and slowly the prairies and forests transformed into a cold desert. Masses of damp sea air must in fact rise higher when they encounter a mountain, where they cool off and cause rain. By the time they get to the other side, they contain no more moisture, and thus a desert is created. Deserts like this exist east of the Sierra Nevada in North America and in certain areas of Australia. But it is not easy to retrace the past and discover the subtle changes that may have created a desert. It is much less complicated to determine why only certain areas of the Earth are so inhospitable.

The first and apparently obvious cause is the lack of rain. The movement of the Earth and the heat of the sun produce a slow circulation of gigantic masses of air in the atmosphere. Warm air rises from the Equator, separates and travels south and north. When it reaches the tropics, it descends back down to earth. Air cools off as it rises and thus loses moisture; when it descends it warms up and absorbs atmospheric moisture, drying out the earth below. If we look at the location of desert regions on a map, we will see that nearly all of them are on one of the two tropics, the tropic of Cancer in the north and the tropic of Capricorn in the south. The Sahara, the Thar desert, the Gobi, the American deserts and the Arabian desert are basically all on the tropic of Cancer, while the Namib, the Kalahari and the Australian deserts are on the tropic of Capricorn.

Other deserts are the result of ocean currents. The result is that certain minor deserts are quite close to the sea. The sands of the Atacama in Chile and the Namib in Namibia drift into the sea, as do those of the extraordinary desert of Baja California in Mexico. It appears that the cold waters come from the Antarctic regions. Brushing against the edges of the continents as they pass, in their turn they cool the air above, thus forming a surrealistic mist that hangs over the coast for most of the year. Very little rain is able to reach the interior. In fact, the cold air passes over the desert without leaving even a drop of rain, and instead releases its moisture in the continental interior when it encounters an expanse of forests or warmer earth.

After its birth, the harsh landscape of the desert evolves, sculpted by the wind and paradoxically, by water as well. The few millimeters of rain that fall each year, if they fall at all, strike bare earth, unprotected by vegetation and easily subject to erosion. Small but lively streams form that transport water to the lower areas. The vast but very shallow lakes that result are soon dried up by the fierce sun; the evaporation leaves brilliant stretches of salts that are inhospitable to any kind of life. They are known as pans or playas, like those which sometimes cover portions of the Kalahari or the Great Basin in North America.

But the wind is clearly the master of the desert. The rocks, exposed to winds and frequent and sudden changes in temperature, assume

14-15 *Desert peoples the world over have had to adapt to an environment which is so hostile and arid that any gesture, any drop of water, any resource, becomes precious. The majority of them are nomadic shepherds who carefully exploit anything the environment offers them. Indeed, nomadism is essential if they are to avoid overexploiting the few riches that the desert begrudges them: if the herds remain in one place too long, they would quickly exhaust the pastures. These images, taken in Kaokoland in Namibia, depict certain aspects of daily life in a Himba village.*

unexpected shapes and break off into small rocky formations. They are finally worn down into sand, which the wind piles up into dunes. In some areas like the Sahara and portions of the North American deserts, dunes are an important feature of the area. In the Sahara and the Arabian deserts, they can reach two hundred meters in height, while in other deserts sand is scarce and the winds are ceaseless. The dunes thus shift continuously, covering and uncovering the desert floor. Smaller versions of these shifting dunes can be found even in Europe, slow-moving phantoms that suffocate all life they encounter. For example, they exist on the coasts of Spain, in the Doñana National Park, and in Poland in the Slowinski Park, as well as on the splendid Sardinian coast of Piscinas. Dune formation is also controlled by the wind. The classic barchans, or crescent moon shaped dunes which add so much to the fascination of the desert, are created by ceaseless winds in a desert without a great deal of sand. However, if the quantity of sand increases, the dunes flow together to form long transverse bands that move through the desert. When the wind blows from more than one direction, star-shaped dunes are formed. Geologists recognize many other dune forms, but rather than classifying them all, suffice it to say that although they are important, dunes are only one of the many forms that wind and water create in the desert. Others include eroded plateaus and forbidding or fantastic rock formations, glimpses of a magical world that changes form during brief moments when water creates ephemeral lakes that swarm with life. All this is the desert landscape, the ecological theater in which, as one great ecologist put it, a different "evolutionary comedy" is played out for each ecosystem and species.

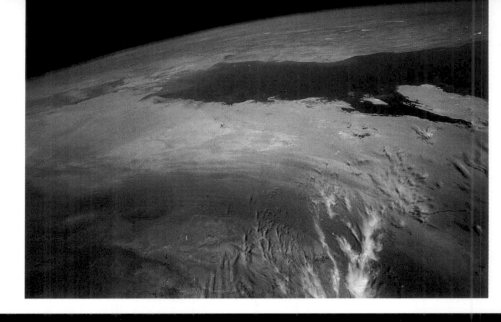

16 top This image, taken from the Shuttle, shows the Arabian desert, with Riyadh below, the Persian Gulf in the center and Iran in the background.

16-17 Irrigation possibilities have changed the face of Saudi Arabia. Until a few years ago only few fields were irrigated by circular systems, but now the land between the sea of sand at Ad Dhana (to the right in the photograph) and the plateau of Nejd is almost completely covered with crops.

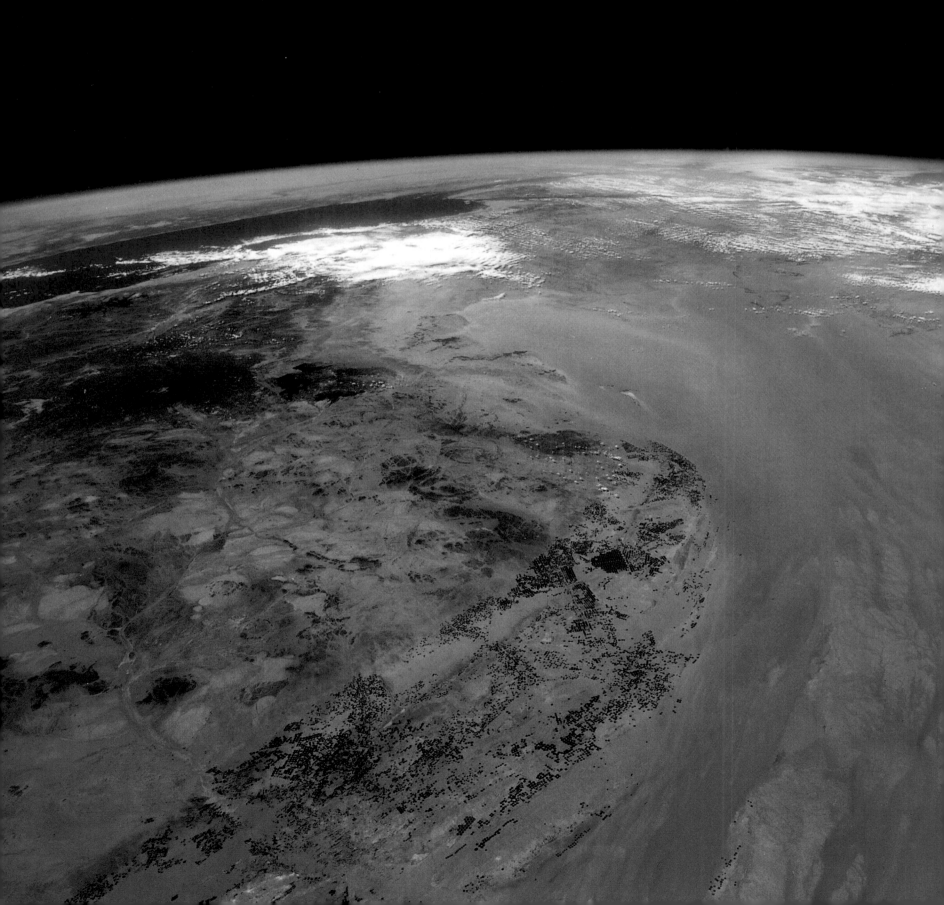

17 top This satellite photograph shows the various landscapes of the Sahara in North Africa.

17 bottom The contrast between the desert and the Nile Valley is evident in this photograph.

20-21 Bryce Canyon consists of a series of horseshoe-shaped canyons about 300 meters deep, with high sandstone walls sculpted by erosion into extremely unusual forms.

22-23 Salton Flat in Death Valley, California, is a wild expanse of salt void of any form of life.

24-25 Etosha Pan is an immense depression in Namibia, alternately covered with either water or salt. When the water arrives, it forms a great lake that slakes the thirst of thousands of animals. After a few weeks the sun dries it out, and the earth is once again covered with sterile salts. In the photo a group of ostriches leaves the pan, kicking up clouds of salt.

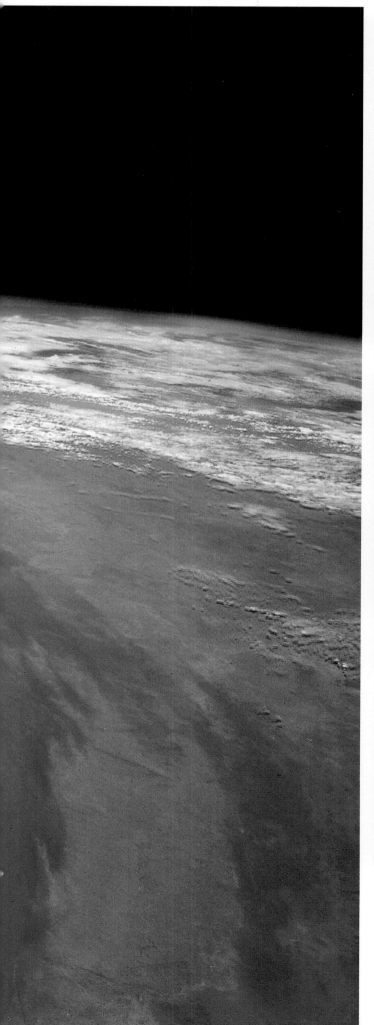

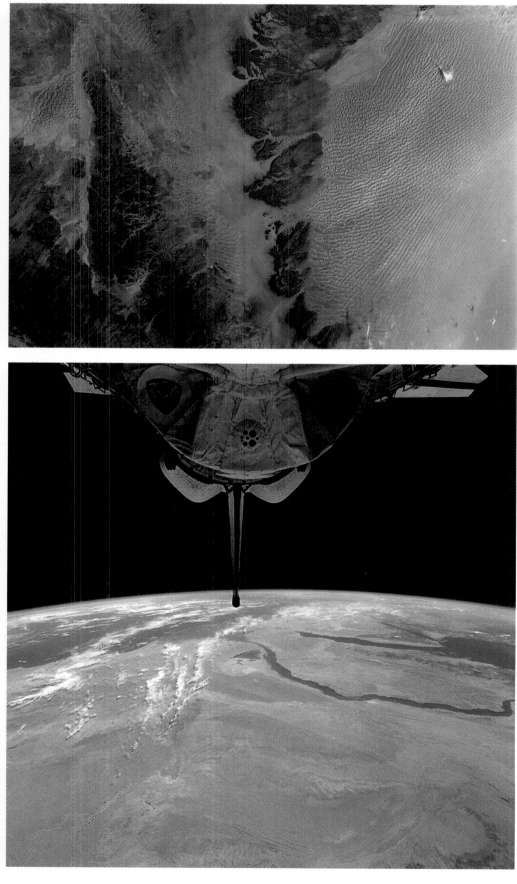

ARCTIC

GREENLAND

NORTH
AMERICA

GREAT
BASIN

DEATH
VALLEY

MOJAVE

SONORA

COLORADO
PLATEAU

Colorado

EUROP

MEDITERR
SEA

ATLAS

TASSILI

Hoggar ▲

TIBESTI

S A H A R A

ATLANTIC

OCEAN

CENTRAL
AMERICA

CARIBBEAN
SEA

A F R

PACIFIC

OCEAN

Amazon

SOUTH
AMERICA

ZA

P A T A G O N I A

OCEAN

SIBERIA

A S I A

BLACK
SEA
CASPIAN
SEA

G O B I

ANEAN

NEGEV

SINAI

HIMALAYA

Nile

AR-RUB'
AL-KHALI

C A

INDIAN

OCEAN

KALAHARI

GIBSON
DESERT

GREAT SANDY
DESERT

SIMPSON
DESERT

GREAT VICTORIA
DESERT

AUSTRALIA

THE SAHARA
FATHER OF ALL DESERTS

They had traveled thousands of kilometers, following antelope and rhinoceros, fleeing attacks by lions and leopards. The African savanna had welcomed and nourished them for millions of years. Now the climate was slightly warmer, making it possible for them to migrate farther north in search of prey.

They were the humans of six thousand years ago, perhaps the ancestors of the same shepherds that still lead their herds across the harsh savanna of the Sahel. After a long voyage they came to the vast stretches of the Sahara, but not the Sahara we know today. Before them lay a green land

where grass grew, nourished by the still abundant rains. These people have left us invaluable testimony of the land they encountered.

The drawings visible at Tassili-n-Ajjer depict with extraordinary accuracy gazelles, rhinoceros, giraffes and antelope, as well as the men and their herds. Then, yielding to cycles that had been in existence for millions of years, it became increasingly dry, the rain shifted to the south or north, the animals that man hunted emigrated or vanished, and the desert took over permanently.

Perhaps it is its immensity, a vastness that exceeds the imagination. The Sahara is considered the father of all deserts, and in fact it is greater than any other arid region. Its nearly nine million square kilometers (which seem to increase or decrease as the years go by) cover a third of the continent of Africa and one sixteenth of dry land. Its confines are well-defined in the north (the course of the Wadi Dra and the Sahara fault) and much less so in the south (where the wide stretch of the Sahel shifts with the seasons and human impact). In the south some botanists draw its boundaries at the point where Cornulaca monacantha, a plant typical of the Sahara, begins to appear. But what we are interested in is the body of the desert, the central portion known as absolute desert. Even here, things are not what they seem. The Sahara is not an expanse of millions of square kilometers of sand. On the contrary, the landscape is diverse and spectacular, and only the great reg, the vast stretches of rocks and stones nearly void of life, give way to monotony and at times desolation. Such a vast desert could not possibly be uniform; thus, in the Sahara there are mountains, plateaus, sand and enormous isolated rocks.

The history of the desert is a tormented succession of very dry periods followed by others in which the environment reflowered as it was nourished by water. Its origins go back to over six hundred million years ago, when the mountain ranges known as the Saharids and the Altaids were formed in North Africa. Wind and water erosion smoothed them until

26 The two ergs of Algeria, known as the Great Western Erg and the Great Eastern Erg, are not the only stretches of sand in the Sahara. To the southwest of the Great Western Erg, for example, one finds the Iguidi and Cherch Ergs, while in Niger there is the Bima Erg, which extends to the banks of Lake Chad. Sometimes rocky corridors cut across the long chains of parallel dunes, interrupting the monotony of the sandy landscape.

27 This photograph shows several ergs, expanses of nearly sterile sand that seem to stretch on endlessly, always the same yet always different. Indeed, the dunes take on different forms, depending on the direction of the winds which ceaselessly shape them.

28-29 The dunes of the Ténéré Erg in Niger still stand in the way of the dromedaries that have crossed the desert since ancient times. Commerce reached its height in the Sahara in the 16th century, when slaves, gold and ivory were transferred from central Africa, and metals and manufactured items were brought in.

this part of the continent was reduced to a shield, a flat and arid expanse. Volcanoes bursting out from fissures created by the birth of the mountain ranges served to enliven this area. The ocean then exerted its effect on this already complex region, invading the shield and leaving behind a large number of fossils. The discovery of dinosaurs in Ténéré in Chad proves that life was extremely rich and diverse. But as the shield lifted it caused the sea to recede, and about 65 million years ago it left a vast plateau in its place, where the forces of

erosion began to have their effect. Alternating periods of dampness and aridity (for example, the Neolithic was initially quite rainy) finally led to the area's present climate and landscape. Nevertheless, the Sahara is a relatively young desert. The entire platform became arid, thus creating a true desert, only during the past ten thousand years.

At least in the more marginal areas, human activity in the form of goat breeding has also certainly contributed to its present desertification, with ravenous goats grazing everywhere. Although very little water now erodes the denuded lands of the Sahara, the other great architect of landscapes has done its part, often quite dramatically. The wind, or rather the winds, can change the position of the dunes from one day to the next, shift mountain ranges, change points of reference, cover ancient settlements and uncover fossil bones. We refer to winds because many air currents course through this region.

The harmattan, a winter wind that blows from north to south through the central Sahara, is caused by high pressure in the area. In the spring, low pressure in the Mediterranean causes the famous ghibli, a warm, dry south-easterly wind that blows over Libya and Tunisia.

The khamsin, an extremely dry wind, courses through Libya until June at speeds of up to a hundred kilometers an hour, causing extraordinary sandstorms.

These winds affect not only the landscape, but also the life of the desert. The heat becomes unbearable and vital liquids are sucked away (just as a wet shirt would dry faster in the wind). Animals, and especially plants, which cannot take cover, must adequately adapt to this factor if they want to survive in the desert. Such a tormented history and such powerful environmental factors could only lead to a similarly varied landscape.

The peoples of the Sahara have names for dozens of different kinds of deserts.

For example, there is the erg, the sand desert, what those who have never seen a desert imagine it to be.

And it is in fact the most fascinating image, perhaps because it is the landscape most unlike what we consider normal. Yet the ergs of the Sahara only cover about twenty percent of its surface. They are particularly common in Algeria, where the two Algerian ergs (the Great Western and the Great Eastern Erg) cover an area about the size of France. The bleakest but most terrifying landscape in its own way is that of the regs, wastelands of stones and rocks transported by the ancient rivers that once flowed through the Sahara. Although they were created by flooding, they have completely forgotten the rivers from which they originated. Researchers in fact consider regs the most lifeless areas precisely because they are the most arid. Most of the regs are in the more south-central areas of the Sahara, where the mitigating influence of the ocean is scarcely felt, not to speak of the equatorial rains.

Mountain ranges which once rose from the sea often cut through ergs and regs. The most important of the true Saharan mountains are the Hoggar and the Tibesti ranges. Exposed to the wind and sporadic rain, the forces of erosion we have discussed have uncovered extremely ancient layers of the desert mountains, even going back to times in which volcanic eruptions created the Sahara. The Hoggar in particular show signs of relatively recent volcanic activity - less than one million years ago. The most ancient granite, however, has been almost completely smoothed over the course of time. Other lower mountain ranges (Aïr in Niger, Adrar-n-Foras in Mali, Jebel Sudan in Libya, and others) often lead into broad plateaus, known as hammada or tassili.

To Western man, accustomed to closed landscapes and reassuring mountain faces, the Sahara seems to be a real mosaic, often confusing and disconcerting. But not for those who live there. Plants and animals have succeeded in finding niches for survival in this labyrinth of rock and sand. Even a simple visit to the edges of the Sahara, viewed from within the protective windows of a car, makes it clear how difficult life is here. The dusty air enters one's lungs and even during the best of times the heat is intolerable. The sun becomes an implacable enemy. How, for example, can plants live, torn between the need to utilize sunlight for photosynthesis and the equal need to escape its ferocity? The problem has been resolved by different species in a variety of ways. The simplest is to seek the coolest or dampest areas or times of day within the arid environment. For this reason the mountains, which are able to intercept those few clouds that do pass over the desert, contain the most life. In the mountains it is still possible to find caves, hiding places and fissures that provide protection from the heat of the day. In addition, many animals basically live their entire lives at night. Although in some

particularly exposed areas nighttime temperatures may drop to 0° C, it is the only time in which the animals can come out without being literally dried up by the rays of the sun. During the day the mouse holes dug under the sand or among the roots of bushes are relatively cool and even maintain a certain level of moisture. In addition, many rodents find a large quantity of seeds in their nocturnal raids that they accumulate in their holes. The water content of these seeds is extremely low, no more than seven percent, but when they are deposited in a damp den water can reach 30 percent of the weight of the seed. They become a sort of precious liquid deposit for periods of scarcity.

32 A Berber woman in traditional clothing. The Berbers, a people with extremely ancient origins, have lived in North Africa for a long time. Their language, a branch of the Afro-Asiatic family, includes about three hundred very similar dialects. Although the Arab conquest required them to convert to Islam, many elements of earlier animistic religions are still an important part of Berber culture.

33 The photograph shows several oases in Morocco, true cities that receive a bit of moisture from the nearby Atlas Mountains.

Rodents, snakes, lizards and birds of prey begin to venture out into the dunes and stretches of stunted bushes at twilight. A night in the desert can be quite surprising: one may see animals quite similar or even identical to those found in Europe. The great eagle-owl of the desert (Bubo bubo ascalaphus) *belongs to the same species that lives in our colder woodlands and mountains. What sets the desert owl apart is its plumage. Instead of the brown of the European eagle-owl, the desert eagle-owl is a delicate yellow-red, spattered with darker spots.*
As careful research has determined, it survives on tiny and unusual prey.
The pale yellow-red color of the eagle-owl is characteristic of all desert animals. It has many functions: it mimics the color of the sand and rocks and does not absorb too much heat.
It is the same color as other animals that live in the savannas farther south, such as the mysterious desert cheetah (Acinonyx jubatus), *more lithe and slim than its relatives, which lives on hares and other small animals, even an occasional gazelle.*

34 -35 *The rock frescoes, pictograms and graffiti of the people that inhabited the Sahara many centuries ago are testimony to a dramatic and extremely rapid change in climate. In these true works of art, the majority of which are in Tassili-n-Ajjer, one can see depictions of ostriches, giraffes, elephants and lions. Nevertheless, as the climate gradually grew more arid, the wild beasts and herbivores moved south to the more hospitable savanna, and the animals in the paintings gradually changed, with the appearance of domestic animals and cows. Rather than hippopotami and giraffes, hunters began to pursue the wild goats that still live in the rocky slopes of the mountains of the Sahara.*

However, it cannot penetrate the deepest regions of the Sahara. It is basically a savanna predator which has slightly changed its body and behavior to adapt to more arid zones, and is not one of the real inhabitants of the desert. In order to survive in the sandy ergs, and especially in the extremely arid regs, many species must completely restructure their bodies. Mammals are not the only creatures that succeed in living right in the sand. The hard scales of the reptiles are an ideal system for retaining precious water. In addition, the body temperature of snakes and lizards varies with the outside environment and does not need to remain constant like that of mammals and birds. The desert vipers such as the cerastes (Cerastes cerastes) or horned viper, have developed a curious but highly effective manner of getting from one place to another. Only two points of the snake's body touch the sand at the same time, and it leaves parallel tracks like that of a small tank. Mammals, on the other hand, in particular large ungulates, must deal with the Sahara in all its harshness. Unlike small rodents, they cannot hide under the sparse bushes or accumulate seeds as water reserves. In an eternal battle against time, wind and sun, they must seek the few sources of water scattered throughout the desert. The common gazelle (Gazzella dorcas), small and quite lively, can live for weeks without drinking. It gets everything it needs to survive from the grasses it eats, although it will drink as soon as it finds a source of water. Gazelles are always in movement, searching for food and water, and they move in what almost appear to be orderly migrations. But the true kings of the Sahara, capable of resisting conditions that few other mammals could tolerate, are the addax (Addax nasomaculatus). Like mysterious apparitions, they emerge form the most inhospitable sands and most parched regs. Their large hooves enable them to run quickly even on sand. Like the gazelles, they do not need to drink in order to survive in the desert. The few succulent plants they find in dry river beds are sufficient. Elegant and ethereal, them seem invulnerable to all harm - if the desert can't kill them, who can? Unfortunately, as for many other animals of the Sahara (such as gazelles, hawks and foxes), man is their most ferocious predator. Extinct throughout most of their reign, they have taken refuge in a few very isolated areas.

36 top and 37 The desert fox, a small fox with large ears and a thin body, is a true example of environmental adaptation. Indeed, its thick yet compact fur prevents excessive water loss, while its very light color has the dual function of reflecting away the rays of the sun and camouflaging the small predator in the desert sand. Its ears, however, are its most important feature: wide and well supplied with blood veins, they disperse the heat of the sun very efficiently, and also act as excellent antennae for detecting the slightest noise produced by its prey either on or under the sand.

36 center A scorpion travels through the sand in search of prey to poison with its sting.

36 bottom The horned viper is one of the snakes that uses the method of lateral movement. Only two points of the snake's body touch the ground as it moves, so that it neither sinks into the sand nor is literally cooked by the heat of the sun.

38-39 This photograph shows the stark contrast between two formations which dominate the Sahara - the dunes, in the foreground, and the black volcanic mountains in the background. The origin of a large portion of the North African desert is in fact due to volcanoes, which began to issue forth lava and lapilli, especially in the Hoggar region. These manifestations covered the lava flows on a very ancient shield, a crystalline foundation that the movements of the Earth had cracked and eroded until the volcanoes were able to erupt.

40 The light of dawn over the silent stretches of erg is particularly evocative. The prevailing winds have swept away every trace of the animals that spent the night out in the desert dunes. In this environment every action and every physical characteristic of both humans and animals is adapted to the lack of water. Nevertheless, aridity is not the only danger to life. The few clouds that drift through the sky of the Sahara cannot provide any protection from the daytime sun that bakes the dunes, nor can they mitigate the chill of the night. Indeed, the desert rapidly loses the heat which it accumulated during the day, causing a significant drop in temperature that sometimes goes below freezing.

42-43 *From early morning on, the sun beats down remorselessly on the dunes of the Chebbi Erg. Nevertheless, in the cooler depressions one can find numerous species of plants and animals, such as small rodents that dig their holes under the sand, especially among the roots of the sparse bushes where the sand is more stable. Many other animals, however, especially those which are longer and thinner, succeed in wedging themselves between the grains of sand and literally swim in the sand in search of prey or in flight from predators.*

41 *Under the first rays of the sun, the dunes of the Asmer Erg become magical. Void of any vegetation, the great sandy stretches are exposed to the combined action of the sun and the wind. Even water often plays an important role in the construction of the desert: in fact, the infrequent rainfall is often so violent that it rips the thin layer of fertile soil away from the ground and can shift large masses of earth dozens of meters away.*

44 top and 45
The Tassili is one of the most well-known mountain ranges in the Sahara. In the Tuareg language, the word tassili means low mountain ranges or plateaus, sometimes with small depressions, known as dayas, in which water may be collected. Sometimes solitary towers of granite rise above the sedimentary rocks, the result of more ancient formations which have been demolished and eroded. Like formations unexpectedly frozen in time, or like petrified rivers, the rocks of the Saharan mountains tell of a period before the desert existed. Indeed, these smooth rocky buttresses have seen the passage of innumerable geological eras and have witnessed the extinction of plants and animals and the arrival of man, the latest to dominate the Sahara. In the picture a man is entering the labyrinth of Misky Valley, perhaps in search of the sheep or goats he left to graze freely.

44 center *Human life in the Sahara is inextricably connected with that of the dromedary. The Tuareg, in fact, spend most of the day with this animal, used as a beast of burden or for its milk. If it were not for the dromedary, humans could not transport salt hundreds of kilometers through the desert or travel from one oasis to another. On the other hand, if humans did not dig wells for water and procure fodder, the dromedaries could not survive in the desert.*

44 bottom *The photo shows some women at an artesian well dug in the valley of Bar el Gazal, in the southern part of the Tibesti region.*

46 and 47 top *Life is relatively easy under the date palms cultivated in the oases, and is primarily devoted to agriculture. Water is pumped from the soil using various methods, ranging from animal traction to the use of an equalizer. A large part of the land is cultivated with date palms, which furnish numerous products, including lymph, which is a thirst-quenching and nutritious beverage, wood, leaves and, of course, dates, for which all Algerian and Tunisian oases are famous.*

47 bottom *Several palms relieve the uniform color of the sands of the Taghit desert in Algeria. Many birds find an excellent resting place in the green spots scattered throughout the desert during the long voyage that takes them from their nesting sites in Europe to the African savannas where they spend their winters.*

Up until some decades ago, animals, plants and dromedaries alone reigned the desert. Now wild dromedaries no longer exist. The entire species has been domesticated by man, who has made them the most common means of transport in the African desert. The Tuareg have a unique relationship to the dromedary. A beast of burden, means of transport and source of milk, the dromedary is the Tuareg's most loyal friend, and in the desert their most necessary one.

The Tuareg nomads may be the best known of the peoples of the Sahara, perhaps due to their warrior tradition and their resistance to Arab influence. Even though they are now Muslims, the Tuareg still retain many of their beliefs dating from before the 7th century, when the Arabs conquered all of North Africa. Before that, the Tuareg were the true masters of the desert. The caravans of salt, spices and slaves had to pass through the central Sahara, where the Tuareg demanded a sort of toll for guiding the caravans through the desert and permitting their passage. These people, now more nomadic than any other, even had a capital at Guram, in Fezzan. Like many North African tribes, their origins are unclear. They are probably Hamites, of the same stock as the ancient peoples who once lived in North Africa and the Canary Islands. They were not purely nomads, because even the fabulous Timbuktu was probably founded by the Tuareg in 1100. They were driven out of it in 1468 by the powerful emperor Songahi, and thus began a life of wandering, war and raiding. The Arab conquest forced them to take refuge in the Hoggar mountains. From this true mountain fortress their incursions against the caravans continued.

The need for survival has profoundly shaped the habits of the Tuareg. The color of their clothing, a very characteristic deep blue, is not simply a matter of taste, but is instead functional for the extreme temperatures of the desert. Even though a dark color absorbs much sunlight (and thus heat), it is also indispensable in order to maintain enough body moisture to survive. The desert sand is kept out by a long strip of

48 top *The photograph shows an ancient tomb that stands near Djanet; the funeral monument was built in black volcanic rock.*

48 center *The mountains near Asseurem have a peculiar layered structure, an indication that marine sediments were deposited over a long period of time. The discovery of dinosaur fossils also leads to the conclusions that the Sahara was once a very different environment.*

48 bottom *The Tuareg live in this arid and hostile environment. Proud and independent, they are the true rulers of the desert.*

49 *The sand changes with every change in the wind, but the rocks contain the history of the land: they are like the pages of a book, if one knows how to read them. These towers that rise up at Alidemma, sculpted by the wind into numerous layers, show the varied composition of the rocks. In fact, the Sahara has not always been so arid. Up until about 65 million years ago, a great inland sea covered its entire surface; the materials deposited on its bottom created the foundation of the present-day desert.*

50 *Still tied to their ancient animistic traditions, the Tuareg are very different from their Arab conquerors. For example, no Tuareg woman would ever wear the veil, and in fact only* *Tuareg men cover their faces, as only in this manner can they protect themselves from the desert winds and be able to breathe when the ghibli or the harmattan raise clouds of sand.*

51 *The nickname "blue men" often used for the Tuareg comes from the bluish hue their skin assumes after wearing their indigo blue clothing for long periods of time. Accompanied by their dromedaries, indispensable* *companions in this harsh environment, the Tuareg travel all the desert paths, which they know perfectly. They live in small and modest tents that are often their only possessions, apart from a few furnishings.*

52-53 *Faithful to the Muslim religion, to which the Tuareg have converted, a man prostrates himself in prayer, his face turned toward Mecca. Behind him moves a long caravan of dromedaries.*

54 Women are extremely important in Tuareg society, as they are the repositories of their traditional language and culture; inheritance is also matrilineal.

55 The Tuareg girl shown here is dressed for the celebration of the sacred Mouloud, a particularly important annual festival for the Tuareg of Air and a time when various tribes gather together in celebration of the birth of the prophet.

56-57 *All the families and tribes of the Tuareg of Air gather together north of Agadez for the sacred Mouloud. The men ride small, temperamental Arabian horses, or else the patient, heavy dromedaries. The women ride to the gathering on muleback, and mules often transport all their furnishings. Mounts are dressed up in festival trappings in order to display the social status and wealth of the families that own them.*
After they have gathered, the celebrations begin and go on all night. The next morning, the men begin contests and races on camelback or horseback. During the competitions, Tuareg from various clans compete with each other. In mid-morning, when the rising sun has become unbearably hot, the gathering breaks up and everyone goes back to his or her tent in the desert, and the next day they recommence the nomadic life that characterizes these last lords of the Sahara.

cloth, known as a lithman, that almost completely hides the face but leaves the eyes uncovered. Even their social organization is molded by the harsh environment. It is based on the tribe or family clan and is governed by four criteria: sex, age, kinship and alliances. Family solidarity and assistance and support in vendettas are the foundations of the Tuareg way of life. Although the slaving expeditions have disappeared, tasks considered beneath those of noble lineage are still performed by the descendants of those same slaves. According to some scholars, their script, known as tifinagh, *is derived from that of the Phoenicians; their language,* Tamashek, *is also quite unique. Because of the environment in which they live, and due to their mysterious appearances and disappearances within the dunes and their ability to survive in the desert, the Tuareg are bathed in an aura of mystery and pride. They have retained many features of their religion prior to the Arab conquest. Almost animistic, highly superstitious rites (with all probability indispensable for life in the desert) are repeated year after year. The songs of joy and honor for the great camel-drivers, or those used in rituals of possession, are sung by women only. This esteem for women is another feature that distinguishes the Tuareg from the Arab world. For example, women have noble titles and own property, and culture and traditions are maintained by women, who pass them on to new generations. Social status is matrilineal, and men, not women, wear the veil. Obviously, the reasons are also practical. The men had to travel for kilometers and kilometers through the desert in search of grazing land, and as we have seen, the heavy blue wool clothing provides perfect protection from the dry air and ceaseless wind. Now that the Tuareg no longer guide caravans through the desert and can unerringly lead one to all sources of water for miles around, now that the entire fragile ecosystem of the Sahara is undermined by economic and political interests, it is comforting to imagine that the nomads, the addax and the desert plants still guard secrets that we Westerners will never know.*

58-59 *The St. Catherine
monastery was built by
order of the emperor
Justinian between 527 and
547 AD, incorporating a
small church built in 330
AD by St. Helena, mother
of Constantine, on the site
where tradition holds that
the burning bush
appeared to Moses.
Located at the foot of Mt.
Sinai at an altitude of
1570 meters, it is
surrounded by an
imposing boundary wall.*

THE ARABIAN DESERTS
THE CRADLE OF RELIGIONS

Connected to and almost suffocated by the Sahara, which borders it to the west, the Arabian deserts may be modified by man more than any of the other deserts described in this book. But at the same time, these arid areas have changed man's conception of life. While gazing at the view (a mountain range, sandy plains, low hills and small oases, a landscape which is not in fact monotonous but is rather a mosaic of many different environmentsand many different types of "nature") we come to reflect on the fact that in this area the three great monotheistic religions of the world were born - Judaism, Christianity and Islam. And each of them focuses on the desert as its object of meditation.

The Jews had to cross the Sinai to reach the promised land, and Moses received the Ten Commandments on Mount Sinai. Many passages of the Old Testament depict the desert as the ideal place for God to relate to his people. Mary and Joseph had to cross the desert during their flight to Egypt. Finally, Christ went into the desert before he began to preach, just as the sermons of Mohammed took place in the desert after his flight to Medina from Mecca.

The desert plays a vital role in all of these events, although it is not always positive. According to the Old Testament, the desert is the home of demons and satyrs, and the place where Jesus was tempted by the Devil. With their deep knowledge of these lands, the ancient Hebrews, and the modern-day Bedouins, some of whom still lead a life not unlike that of their ancestors, would not be astonished by the origins of these lands.

The Negev, the Sinai and the entire system of Arabian deserts cover a shield of rock that makes up the Arabian peninsula.

The western portion of this shield is upraised, and consequently the eastern part is slightly immersed in the sea. It is easy to understand what happened when one looks at a geographical map of the area.

On the coast of the Red Sea, in fact, there are a number of mountain ranges which completely separate the desert from the mitigating influence of the sea.

59 top *Gebel Musa, in the Sinai desert, is traditionally identified with Mount Sinai, where according to the Bible Moses received the Ten Commandments from God. Three separate mountains are clearly distinguishable in the Gebel Musa mountain range: on various occasions each of them has been identified as Moses' mountain.*

59 bottom *The Chapel of the Holy Trinity was erected where, according to tradition, God spoke to Moses in the form of a cloud of fire.*

60 top *In these deserts, as in the nearby Sahara, oases are used for cultivating crops and are places where nomadic shepherds can rest: the photo shows the oasis of Ain Uhm Ahkmed.*

60 center *Like many other areas in the Arabian desert, the Valley of Inscriptions preserves vestiges of civilizations dating back to thousands of years.*

60 bottom *The forest of columns at Gebel Fuga is truly evocative. The strange geological formations that cover many small valleys in the Arabian deserts have often inspired respect and even fear in the people who lived there.*

61 *The architectural style used in cemeteries is a perfect reflection of that used for residential structures, which had a flat roof and few openings toward the outside world. In order to increase humidity and keep the temperature cool, fountains were constructed within homes.*

On the eastern side, which overlooks the Persian Gulf, the coast is instead low and sandy, for reasons which include the fact that the millions of years which have passed since the uplifting have very slowly shifted the sand from west to east. The sandiest area is the terrible Rub-al-Khali, which hostility to human life is almost legendary. Indeed, in Arabic its name means the Fourth Emptiness. As in the Sahara, sandy areas are not prevalent in these deserts. Here as well, mountainous areas and great expanses of stones cover the earth. It was very different millions of years ago, as recent research in Abu Dhabi shows. At that time, six to eight million years ago to be exact, the Arabian peninsula was a land bridge that connected Africa to Asia. The situation was the same as it is today, except that the environment was very different. Hippopotami and elephants wallowed in the rivers that coursed through the forests of these lands, and monkeys bounded through the trees. The fossils of birds, reptiles and fish bespeak much richer and more interesting forms of life. Only a small portion of the biological richness of that time has been preserved, and this has made the ecosystem even more fragile. However, many animals are identical to those found in the Sahara, as the Red Sea is a relatively recent barrier and has not had time to create a clear distinction between animals of the Sahara and those of the Arabian deserts. Among the few species which have found the desert to be an ideal environment in which to live are a few large mammals such as the Arabian oryx (Oryx leucoryx) *and the Nubian goat* (Capra ibex nubiana). *Small rodents are much more numerous, and include the desert rat* (Jaculus jaculus) *and the gerbil* (Gerbillus gerbillus); *however, some species are present only on the peninsula, such as, for example, the black-tailed dormouse and two other species of gerbil* (Gerbillus famulus *and* G. poecilops). *Small felines such as the sand cat* (Felis margarita), *and the desert fox* (Fennecus zerda), *the Arabian wolf and the leopard* (Panthera pardus), *perhaps one of the most eclectic predators on the entire planet, lie in wait for small rodents.*

Of the birds, certainly the most beautiful and characteristic is the houbara-bustard (Chlamidotis undulata), *a beautiful bustard with mimetic plumage when it is feeding or resting, but with spectacular colors during the mating season.*

Then, the male puffs up the white and black feathers on his neck to impress the female, while the suitor struts by with his chest thrown out. But if one had to name one species as a symbol of the Arabian deserts, it would certainly have to be the oryx. It is one of the few animals which is perfectly adapted to the desert. Small and agile, much smaller than its relative that lives in the desert of Namibia, the Arabian oryx is a brilliant white that reflects the solar radiation. On cold winter mornings the oryx fluff up their coats to absorb as much warm heat of the sun as possible. The scarcity of resources results in very little dissension within the group, as when there is so little food it is better not to waste energy in fighting. The subordinate males submit to the authority of the dominant male, who always follows the group, pushing the young ones ahead. Their small size permits these animals to take refuge under the desert acacias (which are also smaller than those in other climates) during the hottest hours of the day.

By carefully avoiding the hottest and driest hours of the day, the oryx is able to survive even in these places with so little sustenance. However, the Arabian deserts are not completely devoid of vegetation. Due to their strategy of quick growth and highly efficient seed dispersal, the grasses have succeeded in colonizing large areas of the Arabian desert, even where conditions are extremely harsh.

But grasses are not the only plants that inhabit the desert. Its proximity to the sea, the extremely complex atmospheric circulation, the rain that falls abundantly in some limited areas of the peninsula, and last but not least the heavy impact man has had on these regions, have permitted numerous plant species to make this place their home. These plants are extremely hardy, sometimes adapted to a very saline soil, other times exhibiting characteristics in common with species in other deserts.

62 top A Bedouin's tent, constructed with strips of hand-woven cloth sewn together, is light and easily transportable, even though it is four meters wide and about ten meters long.

62 center The Bedouins live as they have done for centuries. The fundamental reason for nomadism is the need to avoid exhausting the sparse desert pasturelands. Sometimes the Bedouins stop at oases only long enough to plant and harvest, then they abandon the place forever.

62 bottom A young Bedouin seems to wink at the photographer, while she shows off her characteristic clothing.

63 This photo shows a young Bedouin woman with her characteristic head covering and veiled face, as traditional religion requires.

64-65 Light and shade add a magical touch to the oasis in Ain Un Ahkmed. In Arabia most oases are found in the south, where the average annual temperature is fairly cool and precipitation reaches 200-300 millimeters annually.

66 top *The photo shows the interior of a tomb in Serabit el-Khadem. Clearly of Egyptian origin, these structures prove that the ancient Egyptians were in the Sinai as well. Although they were closely bound to the Nile, the river that drove out the desert with its periodic flooding, during the Middle Kingdom they penetrated as far as Jerusalem, conquering the northern part of the Sinai peninsula. The Egyptians were not the only ones to push into this desert: prior to them the Semitic peoples, then the Arabs, the Parthians and finally the Ottomans reached this strip of land, creating different traditions and ways of life.*

In particular, numerous species of the genera Suaeda *and* Salsola *may be found on the wet sands of the two seas, the Red Sea and the Persian Gulf, and where the soil is less salty, there are even some tamarisks. Far from the sea, the sands create a sort of sparse steppe where, depending on the soil,* Panicum turgidum *or* Rhanterium epapposum *grow. As the altitude increases, for example going from east to west, or from the Arabian Gulf to the Red Sea, conditions are less severe. This is due in part to that fact that mountains provide a cooler climate, and in part to the fact that it rains more here. This is particularly true of the mountains that overlook the Red Sea. Indeed, these peaks capture the already scarce*

atmospheric humidity carried in from the sea, and are thus quite moist in some areas.
*In the higher areas numerous species of acacia grow (*Acacia asak *and* A. seyal*), and sometimes juniper woods form, such as on Asir-Hijaz.*
We have mentioned the influence of man.
In order to understand what happened, however, we need to take a step back several millions of years. Although other hominids had always lived in peace with nature, learning to understand its rhythms and adapting to them, Homo erectus began to free himself of this perceived slavery, and thus left Africa, the cradle of mankind. In order to abandon the savannas where he was born, our more adventurous ancestors necessarily

68 top *Ras Mohammed*
point, the final shoot of
the Sinai, projects out
toward the rich waters of
the Red Sea. The
peninsula is not a flat
and endless desert but
rather an area of
mountains and plateaus.
The landscape is quite

rough, especially in the
extreme south, with
numerous oases fed by
meager but frequent
springs; as one nears the
Mediterranean, the
mountains transform
into calcareous plateaus
which are almost
completely uninhabited.

68-69 *The extreme tip of*
the Sinai, where the desert
juts into the sea, is an
evocative landscape of
stark contrasts: on one side
the harsh mountains rise
toward the clear sky, while
on the other the waters of
the Red Sea take on
incredible shades of color.

69 top *The turquoise*
waters of the sea penetrate
the barren expanses of
sand near Taba, in the
Sinai.

had to cross these deserts and these seas.
And in fact some of the first fossils found are
those on Mount Carmel, near Jerusalem.
Since then, despite the harsh conditions, man
has never left these lands.
However, one does not need to understand the
history of mankind to see how profound the
influence of agriculture has been in these deserts.
A visit to a kibbutz, where friendly people are
happy to show you what they can grow, is more
than sufficient. As soon as the desert sand is
watered its fertility blossoms - in the gardens
and fields, vegetables and pineapples grow
vigorously with just a little water a day.
A thin stream of water flows through the entire
valley, and this resource is used to the
maximum. Just a few decades ago, however,
without modern technology, the tribes of nomads
that lived here battled harsher conditions.
Like other desert peoples, in particular the
Bedouins of the Sahara, they nevertheless were
and still are capable of surviving, using curious
expedients which they have developed over the
centuries. Their language, their religion and
their almost compelling need to move make the
Bedouins appear to be a people who are never
at peace. Bedouin tents, which are still
sometimes of camel or goat skin, are light and
easy to handle.
Made in a single piece, they must be resistant
(they last at least a generation). Cloth is woven
by the women, using colors and designs which
are characteristic to each tribe. Family groups
are not isolated, but rather are part of a series
of intricate relationships with others nearby,
with bonds based on marriage and kinship.
However, these relationships can be destroyed by
disputes involving water, grazing land or
failed marriage plans.
Feuds can result that can last for generations.
Over recent years, many things have changed in
the Arabian deserts. For example, thanks to
their newfound oil wealth, hunters who once
traveled on dromedaries or used falcons now
have much more powerful and speedy means at
their disposal, such as rifles and four wheel drive
vehicles. Animals hunted in this manner as prey
or for trophies have very little means of escape.

70-71 *At Ras Mohammed the Sinai peninsula gives way to the sea, inexorably fading into the vigorous beds of coral that characterize these waters.*

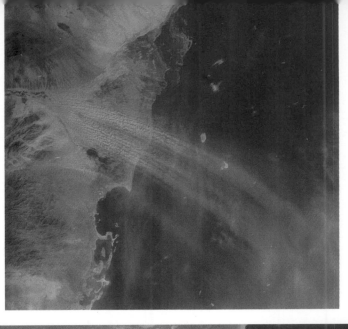

72 top *The dust raised by the strong southwesterly winds hangs over the western coast of the Red Sea.*

72 bottom *Strange, wave-like clouds form at the edge of the Arabian desert, creating a particularly striking scene.*

73 *This photo shows the Sinai peninsula, squeezed between the two branches of the Red Sea and the last stretch of the Nile, one of the greatest "desert" rivers. Indeed, this river carries water from the Ethiopian plateau and the great African lakes through the Egyptian desert to the Mediterranean, creating favorable conditions for the development of life.*

The Arabian subspecies of the ostrich (Struthio camelus syriacus) *essentially disappeared around 1941. The leopard became extinct in Israel in 1995, and very few Arabian wolves or hyenas remain to threaten herbivores. Even the Arabian oryx, which is more abundant in zoos than in the wild, is threatened. Indeed, hunted in every hidden corner of its reign by Bedouins using rifles and jeeps, the species became extinct on the peninsula in 1972. Nevertheless, the situation is not so desperate for all species. In fact, in 1962 the* Fauna and Flora Preservation Society *began an oryx-breeding program that made it possible to reintroduce some individuals into the Sultanate of Oman in 1982, where the climatic conditions were appropriate and protective measures deemed adequate. The houbara-bustard is also the subject of an intense protection and research program carried out by the government of Saudi Arabia.*

Another more ambitious program, which unites the history of culture and religion with that of nature, is being carried out in Israel. In an oasis north of Eilat, in the Negev, where the Acacia radiana *and the* Acacia tortilis *provide shade and food for animals, the* Hai Bar Organization *is reintroducing Biblical animals to their ancient territories. The first species reported in the Negev was the onager, the wild ass that the Bible proclaims to be Pereh, that which cannot be tamed. There are also ostriches on the reserve, although they are unfortunately of the African subspecies, as well as steenbok and caracals, stupendous creatures with slim bodies and long ears.*

The Jewish and Muslim religions that originated in the arid desert necessarily had to push man to "dominate the fish of the sea and the birds of the sky and. . . every creature that crawls upon the earth". The only hope is that man be wise and far-sighted.

76-77 *A dense stretch of dunes hugs the city of Riyadh. The capital of Saudi Arabia is located among several oases in a dry and rocky plateau right in the center of the country. The dunes near the city are one of the characteristic elements of the central region, an area with very little vegetation. After the war oil revenues transformed the city into an important economic and political center. These profits initiated the transformation of the entire territory, with the consequent abandonment of the customs that had bound man to the desert for thousands of years.*

77 *The ancient art of falconry is one of the traditions which has not been lost as a result of the profound changes in Arabia. Long months of training transform many different species of falcons into perfect machines for the capture of prey.*

THE NAMIB
AND THE KALAHARI
THE DESERTS
OF LIVING FOSSILS

The road that runs through the African flatlands divides two completely different worlds. Behind us are enormous rivers, lakes, ponds and swamps in which hippopotami wallow and crocodiles ambush antelope. Before us, just a few hundred meters from the last rivulet of water, lies a world of stunted bushes, thorny acacias, lions and elephants. This is the Kalahari, a fragment of Africa that despite the fact that it is arid for much of the year is not even considered a true desert by many researchers. But experienced in these scorching hours, with a sun that beats down mercilessly on the roof of our jeep, it seems impossible not to call this a desert, this expanse of fine, impalpable clay, with an ostrich running in the distance to escape a thin cheetah, and the elephants that travel miles and miles to find a muddy well from which to drink. Even if this is not a true desert, with no large dunes and extensive portions of sterile earth, the Kalahari is extremely hot, especially in the summer months (December, January and February). Many areas receive only a few centimeters of rain a year, and few species of trees succeed in taking root in the central areas. But its richness of animal and plant species, the presence of tribes that still live in the Kalahari, and its proximity to a true earthly paradise such as the delta of the Okavango, make it one of the favorite destinations of researchers and hardy tourists. In fact, the Kalahari is midway between a desert and a savanna with trees.
Due to the Okavango, it lies between two starkly contrasting territories, the water-rich river area and the arid steppe. Transition areas like this are of great interest to environmental researchers. One can find zebras, gnus and lions, which any tourist in East Africa can see, as well as suricates, striped hyenas, numerous birds such as bustards, sand grouse and roadrunners, and a large number of snakes that sometimes return to the true desert that borders the Kalahari to the west, the Namib. Even the vegetation that covers this wild land (the word Kalahari means "wild land") is halfway between a true desert and a savanna.

78-79 The Kalahari is an extremely vast area that extends from South Africa to Namibia, all the way to Botswana. It is difficult to describe the complexity of this environment: the reddish dunes characterized by sparse vegetation alternate with dry riverbeds, and from the wooded savanna one proceeds to regions covered with black volcanic rock. Both in South Africa and in Botswana a portion of the Kalahari includes vast national parks: the Kalahari Gemsbok National Park in South Africa covers nearly 10,000 square kilometers, while Gemsbok National Park in Botswana covers 25,000 square kilometers.

79 A solitary aloe extends its disorderly branches into the hot Kalahari air. Aloe plants (Aloe dichotoma), very large members of the lily and tulip family that reach up to five meters in height, are truly strange and interesting. The branches extend from a firm trunk and the roots push deep into the ground. The bark is soft and growth is relatively slow. The trunk is spongy, like the American cacti, in order to absorb water during rainy periods and use it during the long dry months. The Kalahari Bushmen use aloe bark to make quivers for their arrows: for this reason the German colonists nicknamed the aloe "quiver-plant."

80-81 *Driven by the wind, low dunes move through the Kalahari. As is true of all dunes, this is the result of rugged earth, a moister area, and a bush or a jutting rock around which the wind gradually piles sand.*

82-83 *These elephants in the Etosha National Park have covered themselves with clay in an attempt to protect themselves from the insects which torment them. Elephants can live in any environment, including the forest, the desert, the savanna and the seashore.*

83 top *One of the most extraordinary plants on Earth is* Welwitschia mirabilis. *It lives only in a few areas of the Namib desert, lost in nothingness. Although what appears on the surface is only a large, strangely-shaped bush,* Welwitschia *hides its secrets under the sand. In fact, the trunk that pokes up from the ground only a few centimeters can be up to one meter wide, depending on the age of the plant. Attached to it are two leaves which may be many meters long. Underground, the trunk turns into a root that seeks out the water table.* Welwitschia's *past is also extraordinary: quite probably it evolved from plants which lived three hundred million years ago, the ancestors of today's conifers.*

As in the desert, there are only a few dominant species, which manage to resist the increasingly harsh conditions. As in the savanna, the earth is often covered with a light blanket of green grass, which herbivores graze as soon as possible. This period of extremely rapid growth of grass during a year which is otherwise completely dry, is the only time when the gnus and zebras are able to assuage their hunger and continue their long, endless migration that takes them from north to south of the Kalahari.

*The dominant plants are the acacias, in particular two species (*Acacia erioloba *and* Acacia haematoxylon*), which are able to grow due to their deep roots that penetrate up to 30 meters into the ground in search of water. This is because - and this is something that the Kalahari and the Sahara have in common - there is water. It is very far down, however, and can be only be reached by deep roots like those of the acacia. This water exists because there is a rainy season that moistens the northern Kalahari, in the area near the Okavango, where about 500 to 750 millimeters of water may fall. The Okavango is the semi-desert's second largest reservoir of water. The great waters of this river fade into a maze of small streams that finally die in the Kalahari. But they do not vanish into nothingness. They penetrate into the rough sand of the desert's outskirts to form the great water table that slakes the thirst of plants able to reach it. However, herbaceous plants clearly do not have roots long enough to reach the water. Thus, they have developed two strategies for survival. During the rainy season, some create a reserve of underground water. These are usually in the form of tubers or very large roots that can accumulate up to a couple of liters of water. Others favor "hit and run" tactics. During the tourist season, the spring or summer of the north, the entire Kalahari seems a dry expanse with no trace of green. But after the rainy season, which arrives - if it does - in January, everything flowers and sprouts and germinates, with small blades of grass poking up in a race against time, trying to produce as many seeds at possible before dying, so that life may continue.*

It is not easy to reach the small Bushman village, despite the excellent condition of the trail. But it is worth the effort. Observing the lives of these small but courageous people for even a few minutes makes it clear that a difficult environment molds character and constitution more than any education. The Bushmen, who in reality should be called the San, once lived in almost every part of southern Africa and according to anthropologists led a simple life that was nevertheless extremely rich from the perspective of social relations. Their territory gave them everything they needed to survive, from the flesh of animals to tubers and roots and wild honey. Their lifestyle, their peace of mind and the relative lack of tribal warfare has led many anthropologists to believe that the San were a real example of how our ancestors once lived. Driven from their land, this population of hunters and gatherers took refuge in an environment that no one wanted - the Kalahari. Despite the fact that they had to adapt to a poorer, smaller territory than their original land, they soon learned every secret of the desert plants. The first mysteries to be solved were obviously those regarding water. Where to find it during dry periods? Expert botanists, the San know all the plants that can slake their thirst. But not all plants that contain water are good for drinking. Some contain a liquid which is so bitter that it is impossible to drink. The San know this as well, and so they use the liquid to refresh their skin. The San's kinship with the desert is so profound that they have even developed an anatomical adaptation to life in an arid environment. Nevertheless, the cultural adaptations to life in the desert are much more profound. The San live in small groups of no more than twenty persons that travel through the Kalahari in search of food. The women gather the tubers and roots which make up a large portion of the San's diet. The men hunt at least eighty species of animals using bows and arrows which are often poison-tipped. Each group has the right to exploit about 775 square kilometers - a vast territory, but barely enough to satisfy the needs of the group.

84 A Kung woman is preparing an ostrich egg omelet. All resources in the Kalahari are used carefully; while hunting is a strictly male activity, women gather fruit and wild herbs, insect larvae and bird eggs. According to anthropological research, their diet is rich and varied, so that the San suffer from very few of the illnesses typical of modern civilization. In addition, it should be noted that the Kalahari has been their territory for many years, so that they are extremely secure in an environment which only appears to be uniform and monotonous.

85 A dung fire cooks the meager dinner of an inhabitant of the Kalahari. Commonly known as Bushmen, the peoples of the Kalahari call themselves the San. They are divided into different ethnic and linguistic groups, including the Kung, the Auen and the Naron. Their language is a strange mixture of sounds and clicks. Family groups have a very hard life in the desert, but know their territory like the palm of their hand and are able to discover resources hidden in even the most inhospitable areas.

86 *Two San climb up a baobab tree to get a comb of wild honey. Kalahari peoples are made up of small groups or bands formed of about ten families each: each group has exclusive property rights over an extremely vast territory.*

87 top left *A group of hunters is trying to determine who killed the warthog: each one asserts that he recognizes his own arrow.*

87 bottom left *A Kung hunter returns to camp with an African python killed for lunch.*

87 right *A child, accompanied by his father, carefully observes the muzzle of a freshly-killed giraffe. The territory of the San was greatly reduced when whites drove them into the desert. Nevertheless, there are still at least 50,000 Bushmen in the Kalahari.*

During the rainy season the groups meet in larger gatherings, to better exploit their resources. Another trick which may seem of little significance, but which is actually an essential aid, is their method of collecting water in ostrich eggs, which are large and extremely resistant. The San hide these natural water bottles on their land, where they look for them in case of need. It is impossible to live in the desert without an inner world that can explain the outer one. And the San have constructed an interesting system of myths which is incredibly similar to that of the Australian aborigines. As in those other deserts thousands of kilometers away, the creator (who is here known as Kaang) created all things, but encountered such

opposition that he left. In addition, the first men created disobeyed the god, despite the presence of two divine sons, who taught humans how to pull roots from the earth. Kaang then sent death and destruction. Even though he has little to do with earthly matters, Kaang is the protagonist of a long and fascinating cycle of myths, during which he has hundreds of adventures. Like other indigenous peoples, the San use paintings to transcribe their world and their desires on stone. Lions, antelope and elephants are depicted with lifelike simplicity.

Although they are not greatly different from the species that live in the true savanna farther north, these animals must deal with a much

88 top *Suricates* (Suricata suricata) *feed mainly on insects and scorpions, but also reptiles and bird eggs. Subject of much research due to their complex social life, they are diurnal animals. Standing on their hind legs, two or three individuals keep a constant guard over the den, warning the group of the arrival of any enemies such as snakes, eagles, foxes or cats, which could threaten their young.*

88 left *A lioness* (Panthera leo) *scrutinizes the horizon in hopes of finding prey.*

harsher and arid environment. The lions (Panthera leo) *often rest under the sparse acacias, and await their prey near water more often than not. When they find water, the elephants will defend it fiercely from any other animal that tries to drink it.*

The gnus and zebras, desert nomads like the San, travel hundreds of kilometers each year as they follow the rain. But while the famous migrations of the gnus (Connochaetes taurinus) *are slow and predictable in Kenya and Tanzania, the herds in Botswana are engaged in a true race against time.*

Certain species found in arid lands are more common in the Kalahari.

They include the long-eared fox (Otocyon

megalotis), *a small, graceful fox with enormous ears that serve to disperse heat and function as radar in order to hear the smallest noises made by desert rodents. Springboks* (Antidorcas marsupialis), *which are perhaps a symbol of the desert, can also be found everywhere.*

They live only in arid bushy areas and carefully avoid the grassy savanna and the true desert. The springbok can go without water for some time, but in particularly dry years, before men exterminated millions of them, thousands and thousands of herds gathered for immense migrations. It is said that the last great migration in 1896 covered an area 220 by 25 kilometers.

88-89 *Steenboks* (Antidorcas marsupialis), *among the fastest animals in the world, can reach speeds of up to 90 kilometers an hour.*

89 top *Smaller but more elegant than the red fox, the Cape fox* (Vulpes chama) *feeds on insects, small mammals and berries.*

Not far from the Kalahari and in fact bordering it and the Atlantic Ocean, is one of the driest deserts on the face of the Earth. The coast of Namibia is the border of the Namib desert, a strip of land over 1400 kilometers long and no more than one hundred and fifty kilometers wide, that includes abundance and desolation and very few animal and plant species, all of which are of great interest to scientists. Just a few hundred meters from the ocean, shallow lagoons dozens of kilometers long are home to dense flocks of flamingos (Phoenicopterus ruber) *and pelicans* (Pelecanus onocrotalus), *who take advantage of the stark contrasts of the Namib. Indeed, the coast is home to one of the richest fishing grounds in the*

90 top left and 90-91
The Sussusvlei dunes in Nukluft Park reveal all the aridity of the desert, making it almost impossible to imagine that the sea is only a few dozen kilometers away.

90 top right and 91
The Namib desert, with its towering dunes and strange and unexpected natural phenomena such as floods and mists, is considered one of the most fascinating deserts on the planet.

world, while the desert is extremely impoverished. This is due to one thing only - the Benguela Current, a cold ocean current that passes along the coast. From the ocean depths the current carries thousand of tons of mineral salts that nourish the beds of algae on the coast. In its turn, the algae serves as food for millions of small fish, the prey of pelicans, cormorants, herons, gannets and other marine birds. However, at the same time the Benguela Current cools the atmosphere above the desert and prevents moisture from being released in the interior. The only time the land receives any moisture from the sea is in the morning, when tiny drops of dew spatter the dunes hundreds of meters high.

92-93 *The stark contrast between the desert and the sea is particularly striking along Skeleton Coast in northern Namibia, a place both beautiful and terrible. Its name comes from the dozens of shipwrecks just beyond the beach.*

This is why the desert comes alive only at night and in the early morning, when the sun grants a brief respite to the animals and plants. As we have noted, very few species live in the sand and stony expanses of the Namib, but every one of them represents a chapter of natural history. Among the plants, the most curious is the Welwitschia mirabilis. Its short, squat trunk is for the most part buried in the earth. The top, bearing two leaves, is the only thing that protrudes. These solitary, enormous leaves, up to three meters long, extend out into the desert like snakes ready to strike. Yet they are one of the plant's most efficient means of collecting the night dew. Their rough, furrowed surfaces serve to "condense" liquid, which then flows down to the trunk. Dew is a precious form of water in a desert as dry as this. A few Coleoptera tenebrionid have developed an extremely efficient method of collecting water.

They position themselves head down, abdomen facing the distant sea. The wind that blows from the ocean transports a fine mist that condenses on the bodies of the insects. By lifting their back legs, they cause the water to run down into their mouths, and are thus able to drink the mist. The only mammal indigenous to the sands of the Namib is the golden mole (Eremitalpa granti). Like other desert inhabitants, including the dangerous Bitis peringueyi, the sand viper, the golden mole spends most of its time hidden under the sand, in which it literally swims. But it does not feed on underground insects as does its relative in more temperate climates. Rather, this nocturnal creature pops up suddenly from the sand to catch any unwary insect it has heard with its extremely sensitive ears. The Namib consists of stony, clayey areas, a few rivers that barely make it to the sea, and low mountains that border it to the east. But the enormous red dunes of the Namib are the essence of this desert, as they are of all deserts on the planet. Soaring and bare, only a very few animals such as the oryx or sand viper will cross them. The tracks left by these courageous creatures heightens, perhaps, the solitude of the Namib, the loneliest, most unchanging, most infinite place on Earth.

94   The horns of an oryx lie dramatically half-buried in the sand. Although the oryx often cross the dunes, their preferred environments are the steppe, rich with bushes, and the arid savanna. These ungulates can survive without water by feeding on wild melons and succulent herbs.

95   The dunes are an ideal environment for the desert snake. To hide itself, this reptile tosses and turns in such a manner that it becomes completely covered with sand, with only its two eyes protruding in search of prey, scanning the surrounding area like a periscope. Even its scales blend in perfectly with the sand: an orange-yellow spattered with small black specks, they are exactly the same color as the dunes.

96 Red ochre smeared over the body is one of the principal characteristics of the Herero, a tribe of nomadic shepherds who settled in Namibia in the 16th century. No one knows exactly where they came from, although they themselves say they originate from near Lake Tanganyika. These rather tall, muscular, agile people consider their homeland to be any place their herds stop to graze. Their life has not been easy since they arrived in Namibia: first there were battles with the Nama, another people that lived there, and then the white man arrived, who could not stand the sight of the unclothed native peoples. Now they are shepherds who are slowly and with great difficulty adapting to Western life. Of the Herero, the Himba, strongly attached to their traditional ways, have not accepted the domination of whites and continue to smear themselves with red ochre and butter and live as shepherds.

98-99 *A small group of elephants heads toward what appears to be an immense expanse of sand with no trace of water. In reality the photograph was shot in the basin of the Hoanib River in Kaokoland, and the elephants know perfectly well where to look for water. Their extremely sensitive trunks have already sensed water nearby. The ephemeral Namibian rivers flow violently for only a few hours each year, but during those rare moments they replenish the precious underground water table that keeps the animals and plants alive for the rest of the year.*

100-101 *Many scholars consider the Namib to be the oldest desert on the planet, and those who have visited it say it is also the most beautiful. Its dunes rise up dozens of meters with their precise, stark forms. Only a few trees are able to grow in the sandy troughs that contain quite strange species.*

97 *A Himba shows the photographer his necklace made of pig's tails. The Himba live far from Hereroland, in Kaokoland near the Angolan border, the first territory colonized by the Herero. Cattle are sacred to the Himba, so that they never kill cows except for religious reasons. They eat mostly milk and wild animals which they hunt with spears. The two groups of Herero stock, the Himba and the Herero themselves, who live in the interior of the country, meet only for the festival which commemorates Samuel Maherero, the tribal leader who led his people to safety in Botswana as they fled from the Germans who wanted to exterminate them under order of Emperor Wilhelm II.*

THE DESERTS
OF NORTH AMERICA
ROCK ARCHES
AND ANCIENT INDIANS

There is something mysterious about the deserts of North America, despite the fact that they have been thoroughly studied, that thousands of films have been shot in the shadow of their pinnacles and peaks, and that even cartoons use them as a rarefied background for the adventures of a coyote and a roadrunner. The mystery lies in both the past and the present, in desert life hundreds of years ago and in that of today, in view of everyone. Even a short trip to one of the four deserts of North America reveals only a part of their secrets. We are used to thinking of deserts as arid, barren places void of life for miles and miles, where animals and plants barely manage to survive until night, when the implacable sun finally ceases its remorseless attacks. But deserts are not like this, and those of North America are perhaps farthest from our typical conception of the desert. Even a brief, casual trip into these deserts can help us understand what richness these complex environments contain, and what mysteries are yet to be revealed. We are heading toward the Las Vegas airport for our flight back to Italy. We have passed some time among the yuccas and cacti, in the motionless stretches of sand and the forests in the mountains that completely surround the Mojave Desert and the Great Basin. The air is electric as we cross Death Valley, and a surprise is always possible. Suddenly, a small herd of desert bighorn sheep crosses the road before us. Their thin, strong bodies, light-colored fur and small horns bespeak expert climbers able to survive in the most arid regions, finding tiny wells of water that resist the heat of the sun. They run suddenly when they see the car, and climb up the vertical walls along the road as if they were flat. After having crossed one of the innumerable large or small dams that dot this thirsty land, we stop to watch the most cunning and familiar of all desert predators, a coyote who watches us from a distance.
Death Valley is the most concrete example of all this. Located at the point where two deserts intersect, one cold and the other hot (the Great Basin and the Mojave), it is a place which Westerners find hellish and unbearable. The first people that succeeded in crossing it,

in search of a shorter passage to the coveted valleys of California, turned to shout "Good-bye, death valley!" to the inferno they had just crossed. Yet for those who are willing to look, there is life in Death Valley, and in the entire Mojave Desert. Every day for six months a year the valley shines silently in the heat of the sun. The clear air and the clean atmosphere reduce distances. Sometimes, for days and days on end only a small whitish cloud brings any hint of water anywhere. The surrounding mountains are what prevents the rain from reaching the valley floor. Two areas of tormented beauty attract tourists to Death Valley. They are the white dunes and the famous Zabriskie Point, which only the shrewdest traveler can appreciate. Attracted by the casinos of neighboring Nevada, everyone goes by at noon, takes a brief look and goes on. Yet only at dawn and dusk do the colors light up on Zabriskie Point or the nearby Artist's Palette. Over nine hundred species of plants live in the valley, with many others in the Mojave Desert, where they take advantage of the rare, torrential rains that fall in the region. They have developed complex methods for extracting water from the earth. Some have a system of superficial roots that cover a vast surface area. Others have roots that extend twenty to thirty meters underground, where they are able to find a little water. Even with this richness of species, however, certain plants are so frequent and important that they act as true indices of the desert. One is chaparral (Larrea tridentata), with its intense smell and small, two-lobed leaves. Despite the fact that it is so common, it has not adapted to life in the desert in an evident manner. Its leaves drop only when dryness becomes extreme, but the buds and young leaves never fall off. It can photosynthesize under any conditions, either in the heat (over 40° C) or the relative cold of the desert winter. It can extract water from the earth even when it is present in incredibly low quantities. It can grow and flower at any time of year if conditions are good. Another species which is fundamental to the life of desert animals is the Yucca brevifolia, or Joshua tree. One of the most recent national parks in America, established in late 1994, in fact takes its name from the yucca.

102-103 *Death Valley is a true mosaic of brilliantly colored rocks and sand of various origin. On its eastern edge at the Nevada border, there are several stretches of sand with evocative and magical names. Zabriskie Point, in the photograph at the bottom, is a small valley covered with sands that change color as the sun moves across them.*

104-105 *Artist's Palette in Death Valley is a true pastiche of colors formed by various kinds of rock. Despite the extreme dryness of the area - Death Valley is one of the most arid areas in North America - numerous forms of life succeed in living here, including moufflons, coyotes, badgers and pumas.*

Joshua Tree National Park is an area bordering the Mojave Desert and the Sonora Desert, and contains the two different ecosystems. In one area, below an altitude of 900 meters, the Colorado Desert, a segment of the Sonora Desert, is dominated by chaparral. The western side of the park is the Mojave desert, slightly higher in elevation and somewhat moister, where the most beautiful stretches of yucca may be found. While chaparral almost completely dominates its portion of the desert, efficiently impeding other species from growing and animals from eating it due to its penetrating odor, the yucca is a sort of friendly inn for many small and large species. The cactus wren (Campylorhynchus brunneicapillus) and the Scott firebird (Icterus parisorum) nest among its leaves; the Gila woodpecker (Melanerpes uropygialis) actually digs a hole in the trunk. But the group of plants whose presence permeates the landscape of the North American deserts like no other species is certainly the cactus belonging to a quite unique group of plants that has adapted extremely well to arid environments. The most splendid example of this group of plants is the saguaro (Carnegiea gigantea). Like other cacti, it is known as a columnar cactus. Indeed, its trunk grows, up to twenty meters in the desert; like most cacti, the trunk carries on the process of photosynthesis. The leaves are transformed, reduced to the well-known spines. But there are also gentle and mysterious aspects to the life of the saguaro. In May and June, the giant cactus produces waxy white flowers rich in pollen and nectar. Unlike other plants, these flowers bloom only at night. Who could be pollinating such a hidden wonder? Lengthy research has finally revealed that bats do the job of pollination, in particular a species of bat that migrates every year from southern Mexico to the United States, precisely in order to feed on the pollen and nectar of the saguaro, and in the process pollinating the enormous cactus. Other animals depend on this gentle giant as well. The Gila woodpecker nests in the saguaro as well as in the yucca, and after the woodpecker leaves, the deep hole protected by long spines is taken over by the tiny elf (Micrathene withney), the smallest of the owls.

106 top The desert tortoise is the object of several research and protection programs, because the changes man has brought to its environment are endangering its survival.

106 center This small woodpecker from the Colaptes genus hunts its prey and nests within the great saguaro, the largest and most imposing cactus species in these areas.

106 bottom This cactus from the genus Echinocereus, which the Americans call cholla, is an extremely important species for the desert ecosystem. Cacti are certainly the most well known of the plants that live in these areas, and they take on a multitude of forms in order to combat the dry atmosphere and avoid grazing herbivores.

107 The yucca, or Joshua tree, as Americans call it, is one of the symbols of the warmer deserts of North America, the Sonora and the Mojave. Its pointed leaves and white, night-blooming flowers are one of the most distinctive characteristics of these regions. The taller, older yucca is one of the most imposing trees in the entire desert, and is found in Joshua Tree National Park. Nearly 9 meters high, it has a crown over 10 meters wide. This plant is believed to be over 900 years old.

108-109 *Cacti are probably the most characteristic symbol of warm deserts. They grow very slowly and even under terrible conditions are able to accumulate dozens of liters of water within their spongy trunks. Over the course of hundreds of years cacti can grow dozens of meters high, standing out in the desert like sentinels.*

109 top *The coyote, ever-present in the myths of the American Indians as the sly trickster, is one of the most adaptable creatures on the North American continent. It can live in the middle of the desert or in the forest, in the snow or in the city; it preys on large animals like deer but does not disdain mice or berries. Its howl, almost like a laugh, adds a magical touch to the atmosphere of the North American deserts.*

The Gila woodpecker is so attached to the saguaro and to one of its relatives that lives in Baja California, that it can be found only where the soft pulp of the cactus permits it to dig its nest. If children are familiar with the deserts of the Southwest United States and Mexico, this is also due to the surreal but amusing adventures of two of the most common species in these arid lands, the roadrunner (Geococcyx californianus) and the coyote (Canis latrans), whom we met earlier. The former is a sort of cuckoo that, although it can fly, prefers to run through the sand to chase prey such as small lizards, snakes and large insects. With respect to the latter, the great ecologist John Alcock said "Why are coyotes so diabolically intelligent and capable of tricking humans? Perhaps their wandering life and omnivorous habits have led to the selection of more intelligent individuals." Coyotes and wolves are important figures in Indian mythology (and not just in the Southwest). Coyote is the trickster, the sly animal that guards the wisdom of the ancestors, who teaches man how to live in the desert but never takes seriously the task the gods have given him. Even now, with his eternal air of a vagabond, the coyote is the most common of the great desert predators. Along with him, but only in the most protected and isolated areas far from the influence of man, there are pumas, bobcats and ocelots, three felines who are perfect predators - perhaps too perfect for man to accept as competitors. Going from the largest to the smallest, these deserts also have an extraordinary population of hummingbirds, or even parrots and quetzals. They all live in a hidden and secret canyon ecosystem, covered with tiny but perennial streams, that furrow the desert. Every corner of the North American deserts holds surprises, species that we would not expect, mysteries still to be revealed and whispers of ancient legends. Looking at the coyote, we can only reflect on the wisdom of the inhabitants of the North American deserts. These plants and animals, like the Indians that live alongside them, are an example of survival in a harsh yet fascinating environment, where men and animals have often found the peace of a perfect coexistence.

110-111 *The Grand Canyon, perhaps the most famous national park in the United States, is a spectacular fissure in the earth, and at the same time one of the places where the history of our planet is most clearly evident. Carved out by the Colorado River, the Grand Canyon is about 349 kilometers long and* *from 6 to 29 kilometers wide, reaching a depth of about 1.6 kilometers. The canyon slices through an arid plateau, deeply eroded by water, in which only junipers and pines grow. At the bottom of the canyon the climate is somewhat less severe, but summer temperatures can still become extremely hot.*

112-113 *An aerial view shows the Lake Powell area, one of the largest artificial lakes in the world, located between Arizona and Utah.*

114-115 *Lake Powell, created by the Grand Canyon dam, is about 300 kilometers long with a surface area of about 650 square kilometers. The lateral canyons, now covered by water, are like* *vividly colored fjords. By navigating the waters of the lake, one reaches Rainbow Bridge National Monument, at 90 meters high the largest rock arch in the world.*

The Great Basin is a cold desert in which the scarcity of water is due mainly to its great distance from the sea and the fact that all the rivers empty into the interior as if it were an immense cup with raised edges; nothing reaches the sea. These rivers slowly dry out, leaving behind a great plateau which is arid, yet extremely complex and full of enormous valleys and dark canyons, red rocks and pinnacles, dense woods and earth completely void of any vegetation. Only the southern branches of the Great Basin are warm, almost like real deserts. The place that most symbolizes the extreme complexity of the Basin, with its great environmental and geological richness, is also one of the most impressive places on Earth. When you least expect it, there it is - the Grand Canyon stretching out before you. From a distance, it appears to be nothing more than a small, brilliantly-colored escarpment. But after you park the car and actually approach it, the spectacle that greets you is indescribable. The pure majesty and scenic beauty are difficult to put into words. Not only its size, but also the incredible mingling of various rocks and colors, completely different in both type and age, make it so unique. A more subtle fascination which is not immediately evident but which is part of the essence of the Great Basin, can be seen in the difference between the territory north and south of the Grand Canyon, known as the North and South Rims. But the rocks are the first thing that strikes one about the Grand Canyon. The history of the Colorado River, which from above can be seen flowing at the bottom of the canyon, provides an explanation for the many different rock formations that make up this natural wonder. In fact, the Colorado itself created the valley, cutting through rocks like a knife until, reaching the bottom of the gorge, it came to geological formations which are at least two billion years old. The enormous job of excavating and exposing these layers required very little time, geologically speaking - no more than one million years. Layer after layer of different kinds of rock were revealed to man, creating an enormous, brilliantly-colored and fascinating time machine.

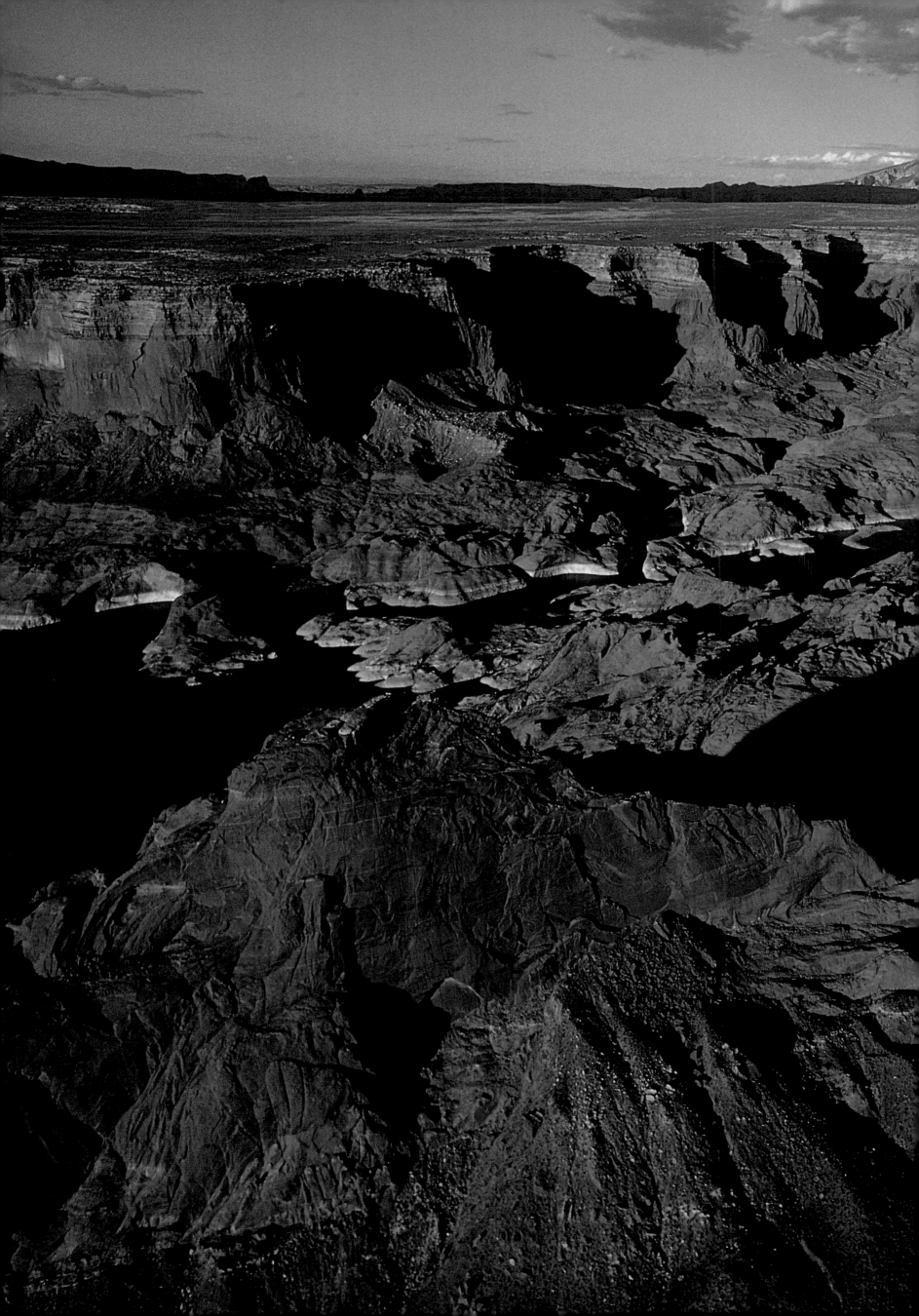

116-117 *Arches National Park includes several of the most spectacular formations in the Great Basin. At Arches, nature has created bizarre stone windows, pinnacles, pedestals and, of course, rock arches: over ninety have been counted and others are certainly hidden in the more inaccessible areas of the park. Perhaps the most famous is Delicate Arch, located in an impressive area of rocky cliffs and enormous rock piles. Geologists reckon that it took no less than 60,000 years to construct this marvel.*

Indeed, a descent to the bottom of the Grand Canyon towards the Colorado River (a trip which can be accomplished on the back of a mule, as the ancient Indians did), is a voyage through the history of life on Earth. Starting from the rocks at the top, which are 250 million years old, one proceeds to the extremely ancient rocks at the bottom of the canyon, which date back to more than two billion years. The Grand Canyon represents over one third of the history of the Earth: its upper layers contain fossils of corals, mollusks, echinoderms and fish teeth. The various formations are also rich in many other fossils, from conifers to traces of reptiles and amphibians in the formation known as Hermit Shale. Lower down, at Bright Angel Shale, 530 million years old, one finds trilobites and brachiopods, species which are now extinct. And at the river at the bottom, at Visna Schist, one can touch rocks which are two billion years old. As we descend, however, we discover that the present is just as striking as the past. And we discover why the North and South Rims are two different worlds. The South Rim is for the most part a desert, with few springs and no running water. Pines and junipers dot the plateau, along with cacti, yuccas and agaves. The animals that inhabit this portion of the Grand Canyon include deer (Odosoiletis haenionus), squirrels and a few bighorn sheep. The North Rim, on the other hand, is cold and snowy - the other Grand Canyon. From October to May it is closed due to snow. The plants, the animals and even the people that live there are different. As the crow flies it is only about twenty kilometers from one rim to the other, but by car it takes at least five hours. This, according to those who love the Grand Canyon, is why the North Rim is so wild, hidden and peaceful. Rain is much more frequent here, and snowfalls of over 7 meters deep are not uncommon. Here there are no more junipers, but rather fir trees and birches. Coyotes, lynxes and pumas inhabit the deep forests of the Kaibab Plateau on the North Rim. Even exploration by white men occurred at different times. The South Rim was first visited by Captain Garcia Lopez de Cardenas in 1540, while the North Rim was explored by Father Escalante in 1778, more than two hundred years later. Both explorers were impressed by the majestic beauty of the canyon.

117

120-121 *Along with the Grand Canyon, Monument Valley is probably the most spectacular group of rock formations in the North American deserts. Located between Utah and Arizona, it covers the central portion of the Colorado plateau. This desert depression would not be particularly striking if it were not for the pinnacles of rock, called mesas, that dot its surface.*

The beauty of Bryce Canyon is more hidden, yet no less impressive than the Grand Canyon. It is a rocky amphitheater in which oddly-shaped rocks create strange images that appear to be walls, windows, minarets, pagodas, pedestals, temples or "platoons of Turkish soldiers with ballooning pants." The intricate forms and brilliant colors are stupendous, as if the forces of creation literally exploded in this particular place for a brief instant.

Yet it was only the forces of nature, in particular continuous and imperceptible erosion by water, which created these marvelous rocky amphitheaters. The magnificence of Bryce Canyon is a hidden world, to be discovered, like its forests, a little at a time.

Another place, perhaps the most well-known and photographed place on Earth, is a focal point of the Great Basin desert. Here as well, erosion acted to reveal layers of rock, creating odd, enigmatic formations. Just as a sculptor draws out forms hidden within rock, wind and water have created Monument Valley. Its power is evident as soon as one enters it, and its grandeur quickly becomes overwhelming.

The ancient rocks of de Chelly clay protrude like vertical walls above the soft schists known as Organ Rock, which form smooth slopes at the bases of the monuments. These monuments are so massive and at the same time so delicate that countless films have been shot here. One of the most well-known movie locations is known as John Ford Overview, named after the director who used it for many of his Westerns. And thus many landscapes of the American deserts have powerfully entered the collective imagination as mythic places, savage and wild but at the same time familiar. Their history and form are an integral part of the life and image of the Wild West.

122 *The petrified forest in northeast Arizona is one of the most fascinating national parks in North America. Millions of years ago, during the Triassic Age, conifers and ferns grew among swamps and streams in this now arid region. The forces of nature changed the climate and the area became a cold, dry plateau. Nevertheless, the petrified trunks formed of agate and jasper are stark testimony to the fact that not even the desert is immutable.*

One of the most fascinating mysteries relates to the disappearance of the Anasazi around the year 1300. They lived in the area we now call Four Corners, where the borders of four states converge: Utah, Arizona, Colorado and New Mexico. Here are the last southern branches of the so-called Great Basin, the northernmost and coldest of the four deserts of North America, far from the heat of Death Valley. No one knows the true name of these ancestors of the present-day Pueblo Indians, but they are now referred to by the name the Navajo gave them, Anasazi. The word means "ancient," or, according to others, "ancient ancestors." But many Navajo confess that the translation is wrong, and that Anasazi actually means "ancient enemies." We shall return to this problem shortly. For about twenty centuries the Anasazi lived in this arid land, and the most important products of their agriculture were corn, beans and squash. They succeeded in domesticating the wild turkey, the meat of which they used to supplement their vegetarian diet. They also went hunting in the territories that surrounded the villages.

In time, agriculture became their principal means of subsistence. Along with it, they developed the immense and stupendous structures that made them so famous and mysterious. In the beginning they built simple adobe houses and underground wells, but from 900 on they constructed enormous villages with homes many stories high. Within, special structures called kivas were used in religious ceremonies and other social activities.

Kivas could be just a few meters to up to twenty meters in diameter. Some of the larger ones were used as gathering places for public ceremonies. They also produced stupendous plates, baskets, ornaments and cloths, which they bartered with neighboring tribes.

At the height of their power they settled vast areas of Colorado, Arizona and New Mexico, developing quite marked regional differences. Then suddenly, within just a few decades, the Anasazi disappeared from the Four Corners area. Where did they go, who are their descendants, and most of all, why?

There are many explanations for this disappearance, ranging from aridity accentuated by the cold desert winters, to conflicts with the Navajo (who called them "ancient enemies" precisely for this reason). A new interpretation is also gaining the acceptance of researchers.

In order to understand why, we need to take a look at the marvelous architecture of Anasazi villages. The large structures needed an enormous number of tree trunks, up to 200,000 in the pueblo of Chaco Canyon alone. Today trees are dozens of miles away, but during the time of the Anasazi this was not so, and they had built an extensive road system for cutting the mountain forests nearby and transporting the tree trunks to the villages. With the disappearance of the forests, the infrequent but torrential rain pounded unimpeded against the mountain slopes and carried off precious, fertile soil.

The mountain water no longer fed the complex irrigation system constructed by the Indians, and it finally became impossible to supply the fields without pumps.

And the desert, aided by the mysterious Anasazi, permanently took over.

Now Anasazi ruins dot the desert, an admonition for anyone who must live in this harsh and fascinating environment, a magnet for those who want to find particular spots where the energy of the surrounding environment seems to concentrate.

The best places to see them are in Canyon de Chelly National Monument, Navajo National Monument, Mesa Verde National Park, and especially the Chaco Culture National Historic Park, with thousands of ruins of all sizes. According to some researchers, the history of the Anasazi is one of the clearest examples of bad management of a fragile, easily disturbed ecosystem.

Other desert inhabitants, however, whether due to biological evolution or to having learned over the centuries what happens when an environment is treated carelessly, have succeeded in living in areas which seem extremely hostile to life.

123 *The steep red walls of Canyon de Chelly and Canyon del Muerto rise up over three hundred meters from the ground. Located in the Navajo Indian reservation, Canyon de Chelly is now a national monument containing ruins of numerous ancient structures dating from the 4th to the 14th centuries. There are also numerous Indian wall paintings which document centuries of settlement that terminated abruptly in the mid- 1400's. The Anasazi, probably the ancestors of today's Pueblo Indians, lived for many centuries in the stupendous Canyon de Chelly.*

124-125 *The great chalk deposit in the Tularosa basin in New Mexico is known as White Sands, and is located in White Sands National Monument. The origin of the dunes is odd and interesting: the water that filled the basin evaporated, leaving an enormous amount of selenite crystals on the earth. Abrasion, water and wind transformed these crystals into grains of sand, which now cover an area 54 by 18 kilometers in size. With absolutely no means of sustenance, almost no form of life can exist in these dunes. Nevertheless, in the morning it is not difficult to find traces of coyotes, deer and small mammals.*

THE AUSTRALIAN DESERTS
THE PASS OF MYSTERY

It is a special desert. Not only arid, not only desolate. The various deserts of Australia are a group of ecosystems which are sometimes unbelievable and always extraordinary.
The first white men to reach central Australia considered it a depressing place. "Here Nature is turned upside down, or else it is nearly extinct," they said. Yet those who truly saw Australia, those ancestors of the aborigines who may have come to these shores more than fifty thousand years ago, were able to integrate perfectly into an environment one geographer has defined as "desert or flood." Aided by the receding sea level, the aborigines reached a continent that had drifted in the ocean for millions of years, developing a flora and a fauna completely different from the rest of the planet. The aborigines were hunters and gatherers in the desert, and here they developed one of the most complex and fascinating mythologies on Earth. According to the Aranda of central Australia, creation occurred during alchera, or "dream-time," in which the Creator Altjira arose from the depths, only to return soon after and lose all interest in man. Wandering through these desolate expanses, he created humankind and the hills and animals and plants. Perhaps these atavistic memories are a deep memory of events that no human has ever seen, like the slow drifting of Australia across the ocean or the formation of continents.
Unlike other deserts, however, those who view the Australian deserts for the first time do not feel that they are merely lonely and austere, wastelands of sand and rock void of life. Wherever one looks, the Australian desert is a true mosaic of different environments, and is thus much more similar to the diverse deserts of North America than to the Sahara.
There are regions similar to prairies, other with a light tree cover, not very different from African landscapes, and there is the great central area, in which parallel dunes stretch out for kilometers in an incredible, motionless sea of sand.
Apart from a few regions, the aborigines live throughout Australia.

126 top and 126-127
The vegetation of the Australian deserts consists of a few plants which are particularly resistant to aridity, and many species which have learned to exploit the scanty sources of water.

127 top *In the more arid regions of the Gibson desert, the dominant vegetation consists of plants commonly called spinifex, which form broad prairies.*

128-129 *The Pinnacles desert in Nambung National Park in the state of Western Australia, is the result of the slow erosion of different kinds of rocks by the wind. The calcareous spires date back to at least 30,000 years ago. The Australian deserts, the most ancient on the Earth, have changed very little from their birth millions of years ago.*

They arrived more than forty thousand years ago (and the latest research shows that they may have arrived even ten thousand years earlier than that), and since that time the aboriginal tribes have developed a great harmony with the desert.

As they did not have advanced technology and did not even need to farm as we know it, the aborigines changed their territory using the means they had at their disposal, primarily fire. Fire cleans the earth and is a "natural" method of clearing vast stretches of land covered with bushes, and leaves a thin layer of ash which is useful as a fertilizer for the subsequent regrowth of grass. These are all effects that change the environment in one way - they make it a better habitat for kangaroos and other large marsupials, the ideal prey for the aborigines. But the desert inhabitants did not live on animal flesh alone. Hardly. Plants were also extremely important, both as food and for other purposes. The list of species which were used in one way or another is impressive, as it shows that even in an area apparently void of any means of sustenance, inventiveness and tradition, plus thousands of years of trial and error, can lead to a controlled and almost optimal use of the area. This occurred in the areas near the coast, where it was not so dry.

In central Australia, in the great deserts with straightforward, descriptive names such as the Western Desert, the Central Desert, the Great Victoria Desert and the Simpson Desert, the main problem, common to all peoples living in arid zones, was obviously finding water. And the search for water has molded every aspect of life for the aborigines.

The importance of water is demonstrated in research which has studied the differences between inhabitants of the Western Desert and those of the Central Desert.

In the latter, which stretches out between the central mountains (the MacDonnell Range and the James Range) and the Simpson Desert, it is somewhat easier to find water, due to certain geological formations that accumulate water from the rare but violent

downpours. After a few hours of torrential rain, the water penetrates the earth and then spontaneously returns to the surface in small pools created in this long corridors of rock. Obviously, having permanent sources of water at one's disposal makes life easier for the aborigines of the Central Desert.

On the contrary, members of the Western Desert tribes can find water only on those rare occasions when rainfall is abundant.

Thus they are extremely alert to any signs of distant thunderstorms and immediately begin a long, slow trek in that direction, following paths that only they know.

Even their initiation rituals, which are extremely important in the lives of the aborigines, become less frequent as water becomes more scarce.

For this reason young people must wait until a sufficient "critical mass" of persons meets before they can be initiated. And they may have to wait for five or six years.

132 *This photo shows the monolith of Uluru at sunset. The pure red sandstone that makes up this formation changes color depending on the time of day. At dawn and at sunset, the red rock becomes vividly bright. During other times of day, Ayers Rock becomes pink or* even gray. *It is thus understandable that this isolated rock has assumed such importance in the myths of the aborigines. At the foot of Ayers Rock one can see the detritus of Aeolian erosion. Casuarina trees and low bushes grow on this bed of fertile material.*

133 *The Olga Mountains, called Katatjuta by the aborigines, are among the most well-known mountain ranges in the Australian desert. They are the remains of an extremely ancient mountain shattered by erosion at the end of the Primary Age, and consist* of red sandstone deposited on a layer of rock dating back to over 600 million years ago. Water and wind then eroded the sandstone, forming true rock islands with irregular shapes. Like Uluru, the Olga Mountains are a sure point of reference for wandering aborigines.*

Then, when the drought is over, numerous family groups meet in a place where the hunting is good.

In this harsh and monotonous environment, any formation that breaks the continuity or acts as a landmark is fundamental, especially in the complex mythology of the aborigines. Thus, a mountain known as Uluru, which the white colonists named Ayers Rock, is the center of many myths of the desert inhabitants. Uluru is located 40 kilometers east of another range of desert mountains, the red-colored Olga. It is an enormous monolith, 867 meters high and nine kilometers in diameter. Evocative and incredibly red, especially at dawn and dusk, Uluru is a magical place even for the most insensitive of Westerners.

The paintings scattered upon it tell stories of real and ritual hunts and legends which go back to the dawn of time.

Legends also surround Wanambi, mythical benevolent serpent who can be called upon to make the rain come. He appears in the sky as a rainbow. According to the Loritdjas hunters, who have lived in the area for thousands of years, at the time of the creation, known as Tjukurpa, the three serpents (Wanambi, Liru and Kunia) had a battle for power.

Liru's lance marks are said to be still visible on the rocks. The great form of Uluru actually is streaked with signs of the massive forces of wind and water erosion that have created other formations with evocative names such as Kangaroo Tail and Brain. Although the vision of the aborigines is highly poetic, the natural history of Uluru is just as interesting.

The fantastic monolith is actually just a small part of an enormous rock that extends for more than three kilometers underground. It dates back to over five hundred million years ago, when a huge mass of sediment accumulated in the inland sea that existed where the desert is today. When the waters receded, they left behind rocks and sand, all dominated by Uluru.

134-135 *Uluru, the largest monolith in the world, stands in the center of the Australian desert. This extraordinary rock is nothing more than the tip of an immense formation that juts up from hundred of meters below ground. When Australia was covered by a shallow inland sea millions of years ago, Uluru and other mountainous formations like the Olgas protruded from the shallow waters like large shoals. When the sea dried up, it freed the rock but also initiated the process that led to the formation of today's deserts.*

136 top and 136-137
*The true king of the
Australian deserts, with
its powerful hind legs
and strong tendons the
red kangaroo can swiftly
flee its natural enemies,
wild dogs known as
dingoes.*

Along the trails used to reach water, the aborigines often see animals passing by in the distance, too far away to hunt. They know their long paws and hopping gait well. They are kangaroos, perhaps the giant red kangaroos (Macropus rufus), who are able to survive in the desert not as a result of forty thousand years of cultural evolution, but rather millions of years of biological evolution. They have had more time than the aborigines to adapt to the arid desert, and now they can survive with practically no water for extremely long periods of time.

If lack of water and high temperatures become a problem, the kangaroo can adapt using other extraordinary behavior. Kangaroos sweat like we do, but only when they move, and this clearly conserves water. In addition, if necessary the kangaroo will lick a small area on its hind paws rich in surface capillary vessels, thus releasing a great deal of heat. Through these and other unique adaptations, the red kangaroo has become the king of the Australian deserts.

It can live in the driest areas, and it gives way to the gray kangaroo only in the wetter areas in the South. They can make do with very little for food - dry, low grasses or small branches and leaves. Similar to ruminants, a kangaroo's stomach contains specialized bacteria and funguses that can transform dry grass into nutritious materials that the kangaroo can absorb. This mass of fermenting grass and sticks can reach ten percent of the animal's weight.

As payment for the hospitality they receive, the microorganisms will even degrade and decompose the toxic compounds that the plants contain.

Like nearly all Australian animals, kangaroos are marsupials. . This lack of competition from other animals, along with Australia's isolation, has made it possible for an enormous number of species to develop, from those with incredibly unique characteristics to species which are at least superficially similar to creatures that live on other continents. It is one of the most famous cases of so-called convergent

evolution, that is a similar solution for a similar environment. This happens for plants as well. Those of the Australian desert quite often have the minuscule leaves and rapid flowering habits that plants in North America exhibit. The most famous species is the acacia, more than three hundred species of which inhabit essentially all the ecosystems of Australia.

When sand is dominant, other plants appear. Stunted, dry grasses such as Triodia form ample cushions up to one and a half meters high and six meters in diameter. When the lack of water and fierce sun combine with the presence of excessive salt, as near Lake Eyre, in the south and southeastern part of Australia, plants of the genera Atriplex and Mairlana appear.

In addition to the king of the desert, the red kangaroo, many other animals manage to live in one or more of the arid zones of Australia. For example, there are many small marsupials which look similar to rodents (Dasyurus and Dasycercus). Like the rats of the pyramids, they are able to extract all the water they need to live from the seeds of the plants they feed on. The strange marsupial mole (Notoryctes typhlops), which looks quite similar to our common mole (except for the fact that it is cream colored rather than black), moves

138 top and 139 *Although these two small desert reptiles have a terrifying appearance, they are absolutely harmless and take advantage of their curious, horrific forms to frighten and drive off enemies. In particular, the clamidosaurus, at left, puffs up its large crest in order to appear much bigger than it really is. The moloch, to the right, protects itself by a crown of nearly impenetrable spines.*

138-139 *This spectacular photograph is of Devil's Marbles, rocks located in the Northern Territory which differential erosion has left nearly suspended in the air.*

through the desert sands. It extracts the oxygen it needs from the air between the grains of sand. Apart from similarities, what is most striking in some of the animals of the Australian desert is their inventiveness, their ability to find solutions that no other animal has discovered. The most curious of these creatures is certainly the bush turkey (Leipoa ocellata), which takes advantage of the constant heat of the sun to incubate its eggs. Its nest, a hole dug by the male, is covered with sand and leaves which collect rainwater. After the eggs are deposited in a cavity dug by the female, the sun triggers an almost continuous fermentation that heats the entire mass, including the eggs. The young chicks are born almost fully formed and run off into the desert to seek their fortune.

As in other deserts, reptiles are everywhere. They are as frightening to look at as they are harmless. An example is the impressively named Moloch horridus, a small, slow, absolutely innocuous lizard completely protected by its coat of spines. Despite its appearance, it eats common termites. Termites themselves are the lords of certain areas of the desert. Their nests, which certain species (such as Amitermes meridionalis) build in a perfect north-south alignment in order to avoid excessive heat, dot the landscape and suggest the profound influence these insects have on an already impoverished environment. In fact, where trees are scarce and the sun beats down remorselessly, they are the primary consumers of grass. The fact that these humble, hidden inhabitants of the desert are actually its true masters is one of the most important lessons that the aborigines have learned over time, and is perhaps the basis for their profound understanding of the land. They are willing to transmit their knowledge to whites as well, so that they too may learn to love this arid, seemingly desolate land on which they have survived for thousands of years.

140-141 The Simpson Desert in Queensland is a landscape of sandy dunes about 15 meters high, stretching out in a parallel direction from north to south. Often some sparse vegetation grows, taking advantage of the scarce water that collects between the dunes. Most of the heavy, quartzitic sand seems to have originated in the Lake Eyre depression. Although it is called a lake, this enormous basin has filled with water only four times over the century. Located in the driest region of Australia, its extremely salty surface is below sea level.

142-143 The Simpson desert is the most arid desert of all Australia, with precipitation which does not exceed 150-200 millimeters of rainfall annually, all of which falls within a 30 day period.

144 A caravan of dromedaries goes off, into the burning sands, sharply outlined against the ruddy twilight sky.